BOSTON

*The Essential Guide to
the Heart of New England*

MARIA T. OLIA

MAPS BY DAVID LINDROTH INC.

ILLUSTRATED BY
KERREN BARBAS STECKLER

PETER PAUPER PRESS, INC.
WHITE PLAINS, NEW YORK

THANKS

For Masoud, Bijan, Kian, Cameron, and Leda

The publisher has made every effort to ensure that the content of this book was current at time of publication. It's always best, however, to confirm information before making final travel plans, since telephone numbers, Web sites, prices, hours of operation, and other facts are always subject to change. The publisher cannot accept responsibility for any consequences arising from the use of this book. We value your feedback and suggestions. Please write to: Editors, Peter Pauper Press, Inc., 202 Mamaroneck Avenue, Suite 400, White Plains, New York 10601-5376.

Illustrations copyright © 2012 Kerren Barbas Steckler
Maps © 2012 David Lindroth Inc.

Designed by Heather Zschock

Metro map used by permission of the MBTA

Visit us at www.peterpauper.com

THE LITTLE
BLACK BOOK OF

BOSTON

CONTENTS

INTRODUCTION

Cobblestone streets and red brick buildings. Swan boats gliding across the Public Garden lagoon. New England clam "chow-dah." The beloved Red Sox. "Old Ironsides," the USS *Constitution*. The "Hub of the Universe." The "Athens of America."

Founded in 1630, Boston is one of America's oldest cities. Sandwiched between the Charles River and the Atlantic Ocean, Boston was built on a muddy little

peninsula . . . and considerable landfill. A bit understated in the very best way, Boston has an almost European feel, with a walkable downtown, charming architecture, and distinct and diverse neighborhoods. Its colonial old town melds well with the contemporary buildings that form this vibrant metropolis. And its newly revitalized waterfront sparkles, from the Charles River to its famous harbor.

This "Cradle of Liberty" is certainly about colonial history. And it doesn't confine its history to a museum. The cherished sites of the American Revolution are all around you. But Boston is definitely not stuck on its past. It's a cosmopolitan city that supports world-renowned cultural institutions and serves as home to more than 30 colleges and universities. As a result, there's tremendous creative and intellectual energy in Boston . . . and a definite youthful vibe.

This book covers the best Boston has to offer: historic sites, landmarks, contemporary arts offerings, varied shopping opportunities, and a buzzing dining and nightlife scene.

The first seven chapters cover sites in Boston's central neighborhoods. Cambridge may be known as "Boston's Left Bank," but it is a separate city across the Charles River, so it gets a chapter to itself. Chapter 9 covers the highlights of Boston's residential neighborhoods, and the tenth chapter describes excursions in New England. You'll find an overview "key" map of Boston inside the front cover and a public transportation map in the back of the book.

A complex blend of both old and new, the "Hub" packs in history, culture, and entertainment. This *Little Black Book* will help you experience it all.

How to Use This Guide

We have included chapter fold-out maps with color-coded numbers that correspond to the places listed in the text. The **Red** symbols indicate **Places to See**: landmarks, arts and entertainment, and things to do with kids. **Blue** symbols indicate **Places to Eat & Drink**: restaurants, bars, and nightlife. **Orange** symbols show **Where to Shop**. And Green symbols tell Where to Stay.

Below are our keys for restaurant and hotel prices:

Restaurants
Cost of an appetizer and main course without drinks

($)	Up to $25
($$)	$25–$45
($$$)	$45–$70
($$$$)	$70 and up

Hotels
Cost per night

($)	$50–$125
($$)	$125–$250
($$$)	$250–$400
($$$$)	$400 and up

GETTING TO BOSTON

Logan International Airport (BOS) *(1-800-23-LOGAN, www.massport.com)* is just two miles outside the city, so transportation to and from the airport is relatively quick, easy, and inexpensive. Hop on the free **Logan Shuttle Bus** for service between airline terminals, to the T (Massachusetts Bay Transportation Authority) *(www.mbta.com)* subway station, or to the **Logan Airport Dock**. The **Blue Line** subway will get you downtown in 20 minutes; most downtown hotels are within a short walk of a T station. The **T Silver Line** rapid transit bus service is convenient for the South Boston Waterfront and South Station areas. A novel way to get to and from the airport to the city is by water. The free **Massport #66 Water Transportation Bus** runs on a loop between the airport terminals, the Blue Line subway, and the Logan dock. From there, the choice is yours. The MBTA's **Harbor Express** *(617-222-6999, www.harborexpress.com)* runs high-speed catamaran service year-round between Logan and Long Wharf—it's about a seven-minute ride. Water taxi service is also available from **Boston Harbor Water Taxi** *(617-593-9168)*, **City Water Taxi** *(617-422-0392, www.citywatertaxi.com)*, and **Rowes Wharf Water Transport** *(617-406-8584, www.roweswharfwater transport.com)*.

Several **Amtrak** *(800-872-7245, www.amtrak.com)* train routes serve Boston's South Station *(2 S. Station)*, North Station *(126 Causeway St.)*, and Back Bay Station *(145 Dartmouth St.)*.

GETTING AROUND THE CITY

"America's Walking City" is compact and mostly flat, so "hoofing it" is the best way to get around! A comfortable pair of shoes will get you pretty much anywhere you want to go—you can stroll from the waterfront through the Boston Common to Newbury Street in just about a half hour. Besides, walking is the best way to discover unexpected sights and pleasures you might otherwise miss.

You'll also find that Boston's public transportation system *(Massachusetts Bay Transportation Authority, 617-222-3200, www.mbta.com)* is terrific—extensive, reliable, and inexpensive. The **T subway system** operates five connecting lines *(see page 221 for a fold-out map of the system)*. Noting your destination is important on the **Green Line** (with four branches) and the **Red Line** (with two branches). Travel anywhere on the system in any direction for the same low fare. Your ticket to ride? The **CharlieCard**. Who is "Charlie"? A hapless guy immortalized in a Kingston Trio 1959 hit recording called "The M.T.A. Song." Charlie became trapped in the T forever because he didn't have money for exit fare. You can get CharlieCards (which do include exit fare) from MBTA customer service agents at T station ticket booths and then load the CharlieCard with value from self-service kiosks using either cash or a debit or credit card. Another option is to purchase a paper CharlieTicket that is available at self-service kiosks at every station.

Both CharlieCards and CharlieTickets are reusable and rechargeable. However, fares are higher when you use a CharlieTicket. If you  have questions, you'll find T booth attendants to be very helpful.

The MBTA also offers **water transit** service *(www.mbta.com, www.harborexpress.com)* to various points from Long Wharf and Rowes Wharf *(see page 87)*; visitors often find this a fun and practical mass transit alternative.

Driving in Boston is tricky. Parking is virtually nonexistent and very expensive. The maze of streets is congested with both heavy vehicular traffic and pedestrians. Besides, Boston drivers are notoriously aggressive! So, if you must drive to Boston, park the car at your hotel for the duration of your stay and use it only for day trips outside the city.

> "We say the cows laid out Boston.
> Well, there are worse surveyors."
>
> —*Ralph Waldo Emerson*

BOSTON'S FREEDOM TRAIL

TOP PICK!

Boston's ★**FREEDOM TRAIL** *(Freedom Trail Foundation, 99 Chauncy Street, Ste. 401, 617-357-8300, www.thefreedomtrail.org and www.cityofboston.gov/freedomtrail)* is a two-and-one-half-mile red brick (sometimes red-painted) path through downtown linking 16 of the city's historical sites.

Massachusetts State House *(see page 28)*
Boston Common *(see page 29)*
Park Street Church *(see page 30)*
Granary Burying Ground *(see page 31)*
King's Chapel *(see page 38)*
King's Chapel Burying Ground *(see page 38)*
Benjamin Franklin statue and site of the first public school *(see page 38)*
Old Corner Bookstore *(see page 38)*
Old State House *(see page 40)*
Site of the Boston Massacre *(see page 40)*
Old South Meeting House *(see page 41)*
Faneuil Hall and Quincy Market *(see pages 52–53)*
Old North Church *(see page 69)*
Paul Revere House *(see page 71)*
Bunker Hill Monument *(see page 78)*
USS *Constitution* *(see page 79)*

Rangers from the **National Park Service** lead free 90-minute walking tours of **Freedom Trail** sites from the National Park Service Visitor Center *(1 Faneuil Hall Square, 617-242-5642, www.nps.gov/bost; see Web site for details and schedule before you go)*. Most guided city tours also cover some aspects of the Freedom Trail too, but you can do it on your own. The trail is well marked, and each site provides historical information via plaques, brochures, and/or an interpretive guide. If you start at the **Boston Common**, once a militia "trayning field" and a pasture for the "feeding of Cattell," and follow the sites in order, you'll find the restaurants and shops at **Faneuil Hall** make a logical (and delightful) stopping point for lunch. And don't leave the **Paul Revere House** and the **Old North Church** in the Italian North End without enjoying a cup of espresso at a neighborhood café. Then walk across the Charles River Bridge, visit the Navy warship **USS *Constitution***, and ascend **Bunker Hill** for its fabulous views. Catch the T water shuttle *(www.mbta.com)* back from Charlestown's Navy Yard Pier 4 to Long Wharf downtown, pat yourself on the back, and put your feet up! In summer, the trail is packed with tourists; to avoid some of the

The Freedom Trail

crowds, you might try reversing the order—start in Charlestown and work backward.

If you have children, you know too much history may make young eyes glaze over. So focus on a few kid-pleasing sites, such as one of Boston's colonial cemeteries. They'll find the skulls and winged cherubs on the headstones very cool. "Old Ironsides" will impress even jaded teens. And a Bunker Hill Monument climb is a great way to burn off excess energy.

"What we want to gain
is tranquility. . . ."

—*Frederick Law Olmsted*

BOSTON'S EMERALD NECKLACE

The **Emerald Necklace** is a linear park system designed in the late 1800s by landscape architect Frederick Law Olmsted, who helped popularize the notion of public parks providing escape from urban life. The city's size prohibited the use of large tracts of land for such parks; instead, Olmsted designed a string of linked green spaces connecting the Boston Common, Public Garden, and the Commonwealth Avenue Mall with outer neighborhoods. Each "jewel" in the necklace—the Back Bay Fens, the Riverway, Olmsted Park, Jamaica Park, the Arnold Arboretum, and Franklin Park—is unique. But they all share Olmsted's vision of meadows, paths, and ponds that offer pleasure and places for recreation in the city's midst. The **Emerald Necklace Conservancy** *(125 The Fenway, 617-522-2700, www.emeraldnecklace.org)* maintains the system and sponsors park events throughout the year. At the edge of the Back Bay Fens, the newly-restored 1883 H. H. Richardson–designed Stony Brook Gatehouse now serves as the park's headquarters and visitors' center.

CITY TOURS

National Park Service rangers offer popular free tours along the heart of the **Freedom Trail**. *(Boston National Historical Park Visitor Center, Faneuil Hall, 1st flr., 617-242-5642, www.nps.gov/bost)*

Freedom Trail Foundation Tours. Their "Walk Into History" tour led by an 18th-century-costumed guide is educational and highly entertaining. Other historically themed and seasonal tours are offered too. *(tours depart from the Boston Common Visitor Center, 617-357-8300, www.the freedomtrail.org)*

Boston Duck Tours. You'll "quack up" at this wacky "turf 'n' surf" tour aboard a renovated amphibious WWII landing vehicle; the tour finale is a plunge into the Charles River for a scenic cruise. *(Mar–Nov and Dec, 617-267-3825, www.bostonducktours.com)*

Charles Riverboat Company offers a 60-minute narrated riverboat cruise of the Charles River basin that gives visitors a unique perspective of Boston and Cambridge. *(May–Oct, Cambridgeside Galleria Mall Pier, 617-621-3001, www.charlesriverboat.com)*

Boston Food Tours provides an award-winning walk through the colorful *salumerias* (grocers), coffee and pastry shops, and wine purveyors of one of America's oldest Italian neighborhoods, with tastings, food preparation tips, and more. *Buonissimo!* New **Chinatown Market Tours**

include a dim-sum lunch. *(6 Charter St., 617-523-6032, www.bostonfoodtours.com)*

Boston by Foot Tours. These exceptionally informative walking tours, including "Victorian Back Bay," "Literary Landmarks," and "Boston by Little Feet" (for kids), focus on the city's historical and architectural heritage. *(May–Oct, 617-367-2345, www.bostonbyfoot.org)*

Old Town Trolley Tours. Fully narrated city tours offer hop-on, hop-off trolley re-boarding all day, plus free admission to the Old State House Museum and a 45-minute Boston Harbor cruise. *(617-269-3626, www.trolleytours.com)*

Boston Movie Tours. Visit filming locations of top movies, including *The Departed*, *Good Will Hunting*, *The Verdict*, and *Mystic River*. *(800-979-3370, www.bostonmovietours.net)*

Boston Gliders Segway Adventures offers 1- and 2-hour Segway tours from the Rose Kennedy Greenway along the Waterfront. Fun! *(www.bostongliders.com, 866-611-9838)*

The Hahvahd Tour. Fun and slightly irreverent "unofficial" student-led walking tours of Harvard University. *(Mar–Dec, tours depart from Harvard T station, 617-674-7788, www.harvardtour.com)*

SEASONAL EVENTS

Winter–Spring:

First Night, December 31. This crowd-pleasing alternative New Year's Eve celebration features cultural, performing, and visual arts, plus giant ice sculptures, fireworks, and a Mardi Gras–style Grand Procession. *(617-542-1399, www.firstnight.org)*

Chinese New Year, February. Enjoy the parade, lion dance, firecrackers, and more. *(Beach St., www.china townmainstreet.org)*

Evacuation Day and **St. Patrick's Day**, both March 17. Evacuation Day commemorates the British exit from Boston during the Revolution and is a legal city holiday.

St. Patrick's Day is a huge unofficial holiday; a parade in "Southie" (South Boston) on the Sunday closest to March 17 features Gaelic pipe and drum corps, marching bands, floats, and politicians. *(www.cityofboston.gov, www.irishmassachusetts.com)*

Patriots' Day and the **Boston Marathon**, third Monday in April. Patriots' Day commemorates the beginning of the American Revolution with re-enactments of Paul Revere's ride; battles in Boston, Lexington, and Concord; and other activities *(617-635-3911, www.cityofboston.gov,*

www.battleroad.org, www.concordchamberofcommerce.org).
(Note: Schools, libraries, and municipal and state offices
are closed on this day. So are some museums, attractions,
and businesses—check before you go.) The Red Sox
play a traditional home game on this day as well
(www.bostonredsox.com). Patriots' Day is also "Marathon
Monday." The Boston Marathon, the world's oldest
annual marathon, starts in the town of Hopkinton at 10AM;
runners begin arriving in Boston's Copley Square shortly
after noon. *(617-236-1652, www.bostonmarathon.org)*

Lilac Sunday, second Sunday in May. The heady scent of
spring brings the winter-weary out to tour the lilac collection, to picnic, and to enjoy Morris dancing. *(Arnold
Arboretum of Harvard University, Jamaica Plain, 617-
524-1718, http://arboretum.harvard.edu/)*

Summer:

Hatch Shell Summer Events,
June–August. Catch a concert
or family-oriented "Friday
Flick." Bring blankets and
picnic goodies. *(oval lawn in
front of the Hatch Shell, Charles
River Esplanade, 617-626-4970, www.mass.gov/dcr)*

Boston Pride Week, June. New England's largest Gay
Pride celebration includes a costume-filled parade that
culminates in the Pride Festival at Boston's City Hall
Plaza. *(617-262-9405, www.bostonpride.org)*

Boston Dragon Boat Festival, usually the second weekend in June. This sporting and Asian American cultural celebration is known for its fanciful dragon vessels, arts, crafts, music, and food. *(Charles River, www.bostondragonboat.org)*

Boston Harborfest, week before July 4. A weeklong celebration of the city's heritage with re-enactments, tours, concerts, a popular Children's Day, and Chowderfest, where area restaurants offer clam chowder samples (and you vote for the best). *(waterfront and downtown, 617-227-1528, www.bostonharborfest.com)*

Independence Day Boston Pops Concert & Fireworks, July 4. The Boston Pops Esplanade Orchestra's concert includes a rendition of the 1812 Overture with cannons in con-

junction with spectacular fireworks over the Charles River. Tip: The July 3rd Pops preview performance offers the same program sans fireworks. *(oval lawn in front of the Hatch Shell, Charles River Esplanade, 888-484-7677, www.july4th.org)*

Free Shakespeare, late July through early August. The Commonwealth Shakespeare Company brings the Bard to Boston. *(Boston Common, free, 617-426-0863, www.commshakes.org)*

Summer Feasts & Processions, weekends from June–August. Catholic patron saints are honored by solemn processions, followed by celebrations of food, music, and dance. *(Boston's North End, www.northendboston.com)*

Fall:

Boston Film Festival, September. Enjoy feature films, shorts, documentaries, receptions and discussions. *(617-523-8388, www.bostonfilmfestival.org)*

Berklee BeanTown Jazz Festival, last Saturday of September. See national and local jazz, blues, and gospel artists. *(Along Columbus Ave. in the South End, www. beantownjazz.org)*

Head of the Charles Regatta, second to last weekend in October. Rowdy crowds cheer on their favorite crews during this international rowing event, the world's largest two-day regatta. *(Charles River, 617-868-6200, www. hocr.org)*

MORE TIPS FOR VISITORS

Visiting night owls need to keep in mind Boston's **Blue Laws**—restrictions that date from the city's 17th-century Puritan founders. Many nightspots (and the T!) close here by 1AM, though some bars are able to stay open until 2AM (with last call at 1:30AM or 1:45AM).

Boston CityPass *(www.citypass.com)* provides admission to five top attractions for one low price, including the **Museum of Fine Arts** *(see page 153)*, the **New England Aquarium** *(see page 88)*, the **Museum of Science** *(see page 61)*, the **Prudential Center Skywalk Observatory** *(see page 126)*, and either the **Harvard Museum of Natural History** *(see page 166)* or the **John F. Kennedy Presidential Library and Museum** *(see page 180)*.

BOSTON'S TOP PICKS

Boston offers a wealth of attractions, historic and new. Here are the city's top picks, not to be missed:

★ **Freedom Trail** *(see page 12)*
★ **Museum of Science** *(see page 61)*
★ **Boston Harbor** *(see page 86)*
★ **Institute of Contemporary Art** *(see page 93)*
★ **Newbury Street** *(see page 119)*
★ **The Public Garden and its Swan Boats** *(see page 120)*
★ **Fenway Park** *(see page 136)*
★ **Museum of Fine Arts** *(see page 153)*
★ **Isabella Stewart Gardner Museum** *(see page 154)*
★ **Cambridge** *(see page 162)*
★ **John F. Kennedy Presidential Library and Museum** *(see page 180)*

> "Boston is what I would like the whole United States to be."
>
> —*Charles Dickens*

chapter 1

BEACON HILL/BOSTON COMMON

DOWNTOWN/FINANCIAL DISTRICT

BEACON HILL/BOSTON COMMON DOWNTOWN/FINANCIAL DISTRICT

Places to See:
1. Massachusetts State House
2. Park Street Station
3. Brewer Fountain
4. Boston Common
5. Boston Common Visitor Information Center
6. Parkman Bandstand
7. Robert Gould Shaw and 54th Massachusetts Regiment Memorial
8. Louisburg Square
9. Acorn Street
10. Cheers Beacon Hill
11. Park Street Church
12. Granary Burying Ground
13. Museum of African American History
14. Nichols House Museum
15. Frog Pond
38. King's Chapel
39. King's Chapel Burying Ground
40. Old City Hall
41. Old Corner Bookstore
42. Memorial to the Irish Famine
43. Custom House
44. Old State House
45. Boston Massacre Site
46. Old South Meeting House
47. Orpheum Theatre
48. Opera House

Places to Eat & Drink:
16. Café Vanille
17. Beacon Hill Bistro
18. Lala Rokh
19. Artú
20. No. 9 Park
21. Paramount
22. Bin 26 Enoteca
23. 21st Amendment
24. Sevens Ale House
49. Chacarero
50. Sultan's Kitchen
51. Olga's Kafe
52. blu
53. Umbria
54. Dunkin' Donuts

"We shall establish a city upon a hill—
a Beacon Light for all mankind."

*—John Winthrop, governor,
Massachusetts Bay Colony*

BEACON HILL/ BOSTON COMMON

Red and Green Lines to Park Street Station
Red Line to Charles/MGH Station

• SNAPSHOT •

Located just beyond the gold-domed Massachusetts State House, Boston's historic Beacon Hill has an authentic Old World feel. A neighborhood ramble here is a delight—picture ivy-bedecked brick townhomes, flower-filled window boxes, cobblestone streets, and quaint gas lamps. The hill's North Slope was home to a vibrant, free African-American community prior to the Civil War; the National Park Service's Black Heritage Trail *(see page 32)* is the perfect way to discover its stories. South of Beacon Hill, you'll find the Boston Common, the nation's oldest park. As far back as 1634, it was used for grazing livestock, as a militia training ground, and for public hangings. Today's common, at once an urban oasis, neighborhood park, and tourist magnet, is one of the city's best spots for people-watching. It's also the starting point for the Freedom Trail *(see page 12)*.

PLACES TO SEE
Landmarks:

The gilded dome of the **Massachusetts State House (1)** *(corner, Beacon and Park Sts., 617-727-3676, www.sec.state.ma.us/trs/trsidx.htm, M–F 10AM–4PM, free public tours are offered weekdays; call in advance to reserve)* is one of the most dominant features of the city's skyline. The cornerstone of this Neoclassical structure was laid on July 4, 1795; it was designed by prominent architect Charles Bulfinch. Its famous dome is clad in copper, gilded with 23-karat gold, and crowned with a pinecone that represents the importance of the forests to the colonies. Inside, in the chamber of the House of Representatives, you'll see a five-foot pine carving of a codfish hanging from the ceiling. This is the state's famous **"Sacred Cod,"** symbolizing the significance of the fishing industry to the Commonwealth. The carving was "codnapped" in 1933 by members of the *Harvard Lampoon*.

Park Street Station (2) *(Park and Tremont Sts.)*, dating to 1897, is one of America's first two original subway line stations (the other is nearby Boylston Station). It's also the main transfer point for the T. Office workers eat lunch in the shadow of the fantastical **Brewer Fountain (3)** *(outside the station)*, imported and donated by Bostonian Gardner Brewer in 1868 after seeing it at a world's fair in Paris. The immense bronze sculpture depicts the sea god Poseidon and goddess Amphitrite, as well as Acis, the spirit of a Sicilian river, and his beloved, sea nymph Galatea.

Fifty-acre **Boston Common (4)** *(bordered by Charles, Beacon, Tremont, and Boylston Sts.)* served as a campground for British troops in 1775. Now it's the starting point for the **Freedom Trail** *(see page 12)*. For travel maps and brochures, follow the path to the picturesque cottage that houses the **Boston Common Visitor Information Center (5)** *(147 Tremont St., 617-426-3115, www.bostonusa.com, M–F 8:30AM–5PM, Sa–Su 10AM–5PM)*. Tip: There are restrooms here, too. The Common has always been a popular place for public assembly. **Parkman Bandstand (6)** *(center of the Common)* has hosted concerts, plays, and political rallies since 1912. The **Robert Gould Shaw and 54th Massachusetts Regiment Memorial (7)** *(Beacon and Park Sts.)*, by master sculptor Augustus Saint-Gaudens, has been described as a "symphony in bronze." The bas-relief sculpture honors the first northern all-volunteer African American Union regiment to fight in the Civil War. The white Colonel Shaw, son of prominent abolitionists, and 32 of his men died at Fort Wagner, South Carolina, in 1863; their story was the basis for the movie *Glory*. The memorial is also the first stop of the **Black Heritage Trail** *(see page 32)*.

Beacon Hill's **Louisburg Square (8)** *(bet. Mt. Vernon and Pinckney Sts.)* neighborhood is one of Boston's most exclusive enclaves. Current notables with residences here include Teresa Heinz Kerry and John Kerry. Bordered by elegant townhomes, the square itself, a leafy park surrounded by a wrought-iron

fence, is kept under lock and key (and only residents possess keys). You may certainly take a promenade around the park, however. The statue at the green's north end depicts Columbus; the one at the south end portrays Aristides the Just, ancient Greek general and statesman.

No tour of "Beacon Hill Quaint" is complete without a stroll along **Acorn Street (9)** *(bet. Willow and Cedar Sts.)*, considered among the city's most picturesque. Tip: Thick-soled shoes will help you navigate the cobblestones. More architectural delights await along **Pinckney Street**, including No. 5, the 1798 Middleton-Glapion House, Beacon Hill's oldest, and No. 24, the "House of Odd Windows." **Mount Vernon Street** is also worth a walk. Its No. 32 was owned by Julia Ward Howe and philanthropist Dr. Samuel Gridley Howe. (Julia composed "The Battle Hymn of the Republic.") And whimsical No. 130 is nicknamed the "Sunflower Castle." Note: Most of these homes are private residences.

Nearly every Boston visitor wants to see the bar "where everybody knows your name." **Cheers Beacon Hill (10)** *(84 Beacon St., 617-227-9605, www.cheersboston.com, daily 11AM–2AM, closed Christmas)*, aka the Bull and Finch Pub, was the inspiration for the popular TV series. The show's opening exterior shots were filmed here.

At the edge of the Common, you'll spot the red brick facade and tall white steeple of lovely **Park Street Church (11)** *(1 Park St., 617-523-3383, www.parkstreet.org)*.

The church's cornerstone was laid in 1809 over the site of a former granary. Three years later, the location was known as "Brimstone Corner" because powder for the War of 1812 was stored here in a basement crypt. "My Country 'Tis of Thee," with lyrics by the church's Reverend Samuel Francis Smith, was first performed here by the children's choir on July 4, 1831. The adjacent **Granary Burying Ground (12)** *(Park and Tremont Sts., daily 9AM–5PM)* is the final resting place of Paul Revere, Samuel Adams, John Hancock, and the victims of the Boston Massacre, including African American Crispus Attucks, believed to be the first casualty of the Revolution. Families might want to look for the grave of Elizabeth Vergoose; some say she compiled the "Mother Goose" nursery rhymes. The nearby **Boston Athenaeum** *(10-1/2 Beacon St., 617-22/-0270, www.bostonathenaeum.org, M–W 9AM–8PM, Th–F 9AM–5:30PM, Sa 9AM–4PM)*, one of the oldest and most prestigious independent libraries in America, has been called "a kind of Utopia for books."

Arts & Entertainment:

The **Museum of African American History (13)** *(46 Joy St., 617-725-0022, www.afroammuseum.org, M–Sa 10AM–4PM)* occupies the **Abiel Smith School**, the nation's first public school for African American children, and is the site of an 1860 anti-slavery speech delivered by Frederick Douglass and the 1863 recruitment of African Americans to the 54th Regiment *(see page 29)*. The adjacent **African Meeting House** is one of America's oldest black church buildings. Get a glimpse inside a free 19th-century African American community through the museum's fascinating **Black Heritage Trail**. Guided National Park Service tours *(summer)* and self-guided tours are available. For a look inside life on 19th-century Beacon Hill, visit the **Nichols House Museum (14)** *(55 Mount Vernon St., 617-227-6993, www.nicholshousemuseum.org, Apr–Oct Tu–Sa 11AM–4PM, Nov–Mar Th–Sa 11AM–4PM)*, filled with fine art and furniture. The museum was the home of Miss Rose Standish Nichols, a prominent author, suffragette, women's rights activist, and landscape gardener.

Kids:

The Boston Common **Frog Pond (15)** *(84 Beacon St., 617-635-2120, www.bostonfrogpond.org, M 10AM–5PM, Tu–Th, F–Sa 10AM–10PM, Su 10AM–9PM)* was originally a salt marsh. Today this concrete basin serves as a summer wading pool, a winter skating rink (with skate rentals and a snack bar), and a spring/fall reflective pool. Nearby **Tadpole Playground** offers play equipment, a spray fountain, appealing mosaics, and humorous bronze frog statues. The Frog Pond carousel operates from mid-Apr through mid-Oct and sports pretty horses, a frog, and a teacup.

PLACES TO EAT & DRINK
Where to Eat:

For a casual meal, **Café Vanille (16) ($)** (*70 Charles St., 617-523-9200, www.cafevanilleboston.com, M–F 6AM–7PM, Sa–Su 7AM–7PM*) is convenient and serves fresh croissants, wraps and sandwiches, and soups. Don't miss its French-style pastries. At chic hotel restaurant **Beacon Hill Bistro (17)** (*25 Charles St., 617-723-7575, www.beaconhillbistro.com, M–F 7AM–11PM, Sa–Su 7:30AM–10PM*), foodies bask in the glow of crystal and candlelight, sipping wine and dining on polished renditions of French and American fare like Long Island duck breast with chanterelles, stewed plums, and fennel. If you do breakfast, you can't go wrong with the French toast with cider-braised apples and spiced crème fraiche. **Lala Rokh (18) ($$)** (*97 Mt. Vernon St., 617-720-5511, www.lalarokh.com, M–F noon–3PM, 5:30PM–10PM, Sa–Su 5:30PM–10PM*), or "Tulip Cheeks" (after a princess in a Thomas More romance), specializes in Iranian cuisine served in a cozy setting filled with Persian miniatures and medieval maps. Offerings include its *morgh pollo*, saffron-seared chicken in tomato broth and basmati rice perfumed with cumin, cinnamon, and rose petals topped with barberries. Try **Artú (19) ($$)** (*89 Charles St., 617-227-9023, www.artuboston.com, Su–M 5PM–11PM, Tu–Sa 11AM–11PM*) if you're craving Italian comfort food classics like lasagna and eggplant parmigiana. And Chef Barbara Lynch's **No. 9 Park (20) ($$$$)** (*9 Park St., 617-742-9991, www.no9park.com, Tu–Sa 5:30PM–10PM, Su–M 5:30PM–9PM*) is so very right for Boston, serving extraordinary Italian/French cuisine in a charming town house setting.

Wait you must at the **Paramount (21) ($)** *(44 Charles St., 617-720-1152, www.paramountboston.com, M–Th 7AM–10PM, F–Sa 7AM–11PM, Su 8AM–10PM)*. Get in line and grab a tray; breakfast and lunch are served cafeteria-style. Evening brings out the locals who come for candlelit table service and dishes like chicken Marsala and steak frites.

Bars & Nightlife:

Beacon Hill offers a few good nightlife options. Modish Italian wine bar **Bin 26 Enoteca (22)** *(26 Charles St., 617-723-5939, www.bin26.com, M–Th noon–10PM, F noon–11PM, Sa 11AM–11PM, Su 11AM–10PM)* features 50 wines by the glass and nearly 200 by the bottle, along with an eclectic seasonal menu. The popular **21st Amendment (23)** *(150 Bowdoin St., 617-227-7100, www.21stboston.com, daily 11:30AM–2AM)* packs in regulars from the financial district and state house, and offers a casual American lunch and dinner menu. It's said JFK penned speeches by the back fireplace.

The **Sevens Ale House (24)** *(77 Charles St., 617-523-9074, M–Sa 11:30AM–1AM, Su noon–1AM)* has tons of character, an unpretentious vibe, and is easy on the wallet.

WHERE TO SHOP

Antiquers converge on charming Charles Street. Tip: Antique shops are generally closed Sundays and Mondays. Start your treasure hunt at **Devonia: Antiques for Dining (25)** *(15 Charles St., 617-523-8313, www.devonia-antiques.com, M–Sa 11AM–5PM, Su noon–5PM)*. Its collection of English porcelain and American and European stemware from 1880 to 1920 includes Minton, Baccarat,

Steuben, and more; many pieces are museum-quality. **Twentieth Century Limited (26)** *(73 Charles St., 617-742-1031, www.boston-vintagejewelry.com, M–Sa 11AM–6PM, Su noon–5PM)* is a treasure trove of vintage costume jewelry and accessories; and much of it is affordable. Collectors and history buffs favor the antique prints and maps at **Eugene Galleries (27)** *(76 Charles St., 617-227-3062, M–Sa 11AM–6PM, Su noon–6PM)*. **Caswell Galleries (28)** *(31 Charles St., 617-523-9868, www.caswellgalleries.com, M–W, F–Sa 10AM–6PM, Th 11AM–7PM, Su noon–6PM)* offers framed and unframed Boston-themed artwork and prints.

Look beyond Antique Row for unique shops like **Flat of the Hill (29)** *(60 Charles St., 617-619-9977, www.flatof thehill.com, Tu–F 11AM–6PM, Sa 10AM–5PM, Su noon–5PM, closed Su in Jan and Aug)*, just the place for cute purses, cards, candles, bath and body products, and pretty accessories for home and wardrobe. **Blackstone's of Beacon Hill (30)** *(46 Charles St., 617-227-4646, www.blackstonesbeaconhill.com, M–W, F 10AM–6:30PM, Th 10AM–7PM, Sa 10AM–6PM, Su 11AM–5PM)* sells collectibles, gourmet items, and artisan-made New England pottery. **Rugg Road Paper Company (31)** *(105 Charles St., 617-742-0002, www.ruggroad paper.com, M–W, F, Sa 10AM–6PM, Th 10AM–7PM, Su noon–5PM)* stocks handmade and decorative papers. **Helen's Leather Shop (32)** *(110 Charles St., 617-742-2077, www.helensleather.com, M–W 10AM–6PM, Th noon–8PM, F–Sa 10AM–6PM, Su noon–6PM)*, with its cowboy boots and Western wear, imbues Beantown with a bit of Texas.

Other shops deserving of a rummage are **Upstairs Downstairs (33)** *(93 Charles St., 617-367-1950, M–Sa 11AM–6PM, Su noon–5PM)*, with room after room of quality finds, and **Danish Country European and Asian Antiques (34)** *(138 Charles St., 617-227-1804, www.europeanstyleantiques.com, M–F 10:30AM–6PM, Sa–Su 10:30AM–5PM)*. A true find, the store is packed with a mix of authentic Scandinavian and Asian antiques.

WHERE TO STAY

Thinking about staying on the "Hill"? Consider the **XV Beacon (35)** *($$$$) (15 Beacon St., 617-670-1500, www.xvbeacon.com)*. This Beaux Arts boutique hotel is one of the city's most luxurious. Posh rooms offer traditional elegance with a soft, modern edge, and appointments include gas fireplaces, poster beds, and rain forest showerheads. Or let the **Charles Street Inn (36)** *($$$) (94 Charles St., 617-314-8900, www.charlesstreetinn.com)* pamper you. Its nine Victorian-themed rooms feature period accents, views, fireplaces, and a spa-quality bathroom. The Louisa May Alcott Room charms with a celery-and-rose color scheme, queen bed, and fainting couch. The Oliver Wendell Holmes room impresses with a king sleigh bed and walnut rolltop desk. **Beacon Hill Hotel & Bistro (37)** *($$$) (25 Charles St., 617-723-7575, www.beaconhillhotel.com)* provides another town house option, with cozy, comfortable rooms (all totally renovated in 2011), modern amenities (flat-screen TVs, high-speed Internet access), and reasonable rates that include breakfast in the hotel's hit bistro *(see page 33)*.

DOWNTOWN/ FINANCIAL DISTRICT

Green and Blue Lines to Government Center Station
Orange and Blue Lines to State Street Station
Red, Orange, or Silver Line to
Downtown Crossing Station

• SNAPSHOT •

You'll discover a number of important colonial-era sites amid the department stores and skyscrapers of Boston's downtown and financial districts. These neighborhoods teem with shoppers and office workers during the week, which means there are lots of great mealtime options available for tourists. After five, the business crowd keeps things lively at bars and restaurants. There's a smattering of good hotels here, too, catering to Monday-through-Friday clients as well as weekend visitors seeking a quiet central location.

PLACES TO SEE
Landmarks:

When Boston's Puritans refused to sell their land for an Anglican church to be built here, King James II ordered a section of the city's oldest burying ground seized for the Church of England. The result: the imposing granite

King's Chapel (38) *(corner School and Tremont Sts., 617-523-1749, www.kings-chapel.org, visitor hours vary; check Web site before you go)*, established in 1686. Today, services and concerts are held here several times a week. The adjacent Puritan **King's Chapel Burying Ground (39)** *(Tremont and School Sts., daily 9AM–5PM)* dates from 1630 and contains the gravesites of early settlers, including John Winthrop, first colonial governor, Elizabeth Paine (who inspired the character Hester Prynne in Nathaniel Hawthorne's *The Scarlet Letter*), and little-known hero William Dawes, who, along with Paul Revere, rode to warn of the British invasion. It's also the final resting place of Mary Chilton, first woman to step off the *Mayflower*, and Hezekiah Usher, the colony's first printer.

With its ornamented columns, mansard roof, and projecting central bay, Boston's **Old City Hall (40)** *(45 School St.)* is a nice example of the French Second Empire architecture. In front of the hall, you'll spot a fanciful, hopscotch-patterned **sidewalk mosaic** that marks the site of America's first public school, **Boston Latin**, established in 1635. The school's most famous dropout: **Benjamin Franklin**; he is commemorated by a bronze statue here. You'll find a bit of local political humor in the hall courtyard, too: a full-size **donkey statue** representing the Democratic Party, with a plaque explaining the origins of the symbol.

Originally an early 18th-century apothecary, the gambrel-roofed **Old Corner Bookstore (41)** *(3 School St.)* became the hub of American literature when Ticknor and Fields began publishing and selling books and magazines here 150 years later, including *Walden*, *The Scarlet Letter*, and the *Atlantic Monthly*. Writers who frequented the premises included Henry David Thoreau, Ralph Waldo Emerson, Louisa May Alcott, Harriet Beecher Stowe, Nathaniel Hawthorne, Charles Dickens, and Willa Cather. Now the building houses a franchise of Chipotle Mexican Grill.

The **Memorial to the Irish Famine (42)** *(corner Washington and School Sts.)* consists of two life-sized sculptures—one of a destitute family leaving Ireland, another of a hopeful family arriving in Boston. A tribute to the city's Irish heritage, the memorial is located just blocks away from where famine refugees first crowded into tenements along the waterfront. The famine, which lasted from 1845 to 1850, began with a series of potato crop failures. More than a million fled Ireland, with an estimated 100,000 heading to Boston. Here the Irish faced further hardship and harassment, but the "Famine Generation" managed to recover and take its place in American history.

Customs inspectors kept track of cargo coming by sea at the original 1849 **Custom House (43)** *(3 McKinley Sq.)*, styled after a Greek temple. When the 16-story clock tower was added in 1915, the building became Boston's first skyscraper. Today it's a Marriott hotel *(see page 45)*. The public is welcome to view its historical exhibits *(lobby and one floor above)*; guided visits of its 26th-floor observation deck are also available *(call 617-310-6300 for tour information)*.

Built in 1713, the **Old State House (44)** *(206 Washington St., 617-720-1713, www.bostonhistory.org, daily Jan 9AM–4PM, Feb–Jun and Sep–Dec 9AM–5PM, Jul–Aug 9AM–6PM, closed New Year's, Thanksgiving, Christmas, and first week in Feb)* is the oldest surviving public building in Boston. A symbol of the Royal Governor's authority—the replica statues of lion and unicorn atop the building's gables represent the crown—the house was the seat of colonial government, the site of revolutionary discourse, and a merchant exchange. The Declaration of Independence was first read from its balcony on July 18, 1776, and has been read from here every year since on Independence Day. The building is now a Bostonian Society history museum. The **Boston Massacre Site (45)** *(Devonshire and State St. intersection)*, in front of the **Old State House (44)**, marks a pivotal event in the American Revolution. It was here on March 5, 1770, that British soldiers fired upon an agitated mob of colonists, resulting in five civilian deaths. The circle of granite cobblestones marking the site has recently moved from its former perilous traffic island location to the sidewalk near the Old State House. A bronze border emblazoned with date of the massacre now surrounds the restored marker.

The Freedom Trail

OLD STATE HOUSE

The **Old South Meeting House (46)** *(310 Washington St., 617-482-6439, www.oldsouthmeetinghouse.org, daily Apr–Oct 9:30AM–5PM, Nov–Mar 10AM–4PM)*, built in 1729, is Boston's second oldest church. It was also ground zero for that famous act of civil disobedience, the Boston Tea Party. In December 1773, over 5,000 gathered here to protest the British tea tax; after hours of debate, they proceeded to the harbor and dumped three shiploads of tea. You can attend and participate in re-creations of the debates here, enjoy programs and exhibits, and even see a sample of the famous tea.

Arts & Entertainment:

Coldplay and other top bands often play the **Orpheum Theatre (47)** *(1 Hamilton Pl., 617-482-0106, www.orpheumtheatreboston.com, box office M–Sa 10AM–5PM)*. This 1852 music hall is still a class act. But the city's most ornate performance venue is the **Opera House (48)** *(539 Washington St., 617-259-3400, www.bostonoperahouse.com; box office M–F 10AM–5PM or until show-time on performance nights)*, which hosts Broadway shows, guests such as Maya Angelou, and is now the perma-nent performance home of the Boston Ballet.

PLACES TO EAT & DRINK
Where to Eat:

Crowded storefront **Chacarero (49) ($)** *(101 Arch St., 617-542-0392, www. chacarero.com, M–F 8AM–6PM)* makes one thing exceedingly well: *chacareros,* Chilean sandwiches made of grilled chicken or beef, muenster cheese, avocado, tomatoes, hot sauce, and green beans. Addictive! Another neighborhood non-burger option: **Sultan's Kitchen (50) ($)** *(116 State St., 617-570-9009, www.sultans-kitchen.com, M–F 11AM–5:30PM, Sa 11AM–4PM)*, specializing in Turkish cuisine, from chicken pilaf to weekly specials like *hunkar begendi,* "Sultan's Delight," lamb shank braised with tomatoes and herbs over smoky eggplant puree. For fun flavored coffee and a breakfast sandwich to go, try locally-owned **Olga's Kafe (51) ($)** *(inside 99 Summer St. lobby, 617-204-9809, open M–F during business hours)*, cash only. Located on the fourth floor of the Sports Club/LA, **blu (52) ($$)** *(4 Avery St., 617-375-8550, www.blurestaurant.com, M–Th 11:30AM–2:30PM, 5PM–10PM, F 11:30AM–2:30PM, 5PM–10:30PM, Sa 5PM–10:30PM, café M–F 6AM–10:30PM, Sa–Su 7AM–7:30PM)* is all about the cityscape views from its floor-to-ceiling windows and its healthy menu, with items like grilled swordfish with polenta and broccoli

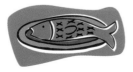

rabe. After-workout refreshments include the "Nutty Java Blast Smoothie." After-work cocktails include "Verbena Mint Lemonade."

At **Umbria (53) ($$$)** *(295 Franklin St., 617-338-1000, www.umbriaristorante.com, M–F 11:30AM–2:30PM, 5:30PM–11PM, Sa 5PM–11PM, nightclub F–Sa 10PM–2AM)*, expect earthy dishes from the "heart of Italy," such as artisanal pasta like tagliatelle with wild mushrooms and fresh truffle shavings, deftly prepared and served in a sophisticated setting. Late, late night, the third, fourth, and fifth floors of the restaurant transform into a swank nightclub.

Get a morning jump-start or afternoon pick-me-up at the local **Dunkin' Donuts (54) ($)** *(235 Washington St., 617-248-1987, daily 5AM–9PM)*. Dunkin' coffee and doughnuts have been a ritual for New Englanders since the company's 1950 founding in Quincy, Massachusetts. For a quick lunch, follow the "suits" to one of the many sausage, burrito, or kebab pushcart vendors on Washington Street. Tip: You'll find the best food at the pushcart with the longest line. Boston has few kosher restaurants; one is **Milk Street Café (55) ($)** *(50 Milk St., 617-542-3663, www.boston.milkstreet cafe.com, M–F 7AM–3PM)*, which has a huge following for its convivial cafeteria setting and appealing menu of salads, soups, sandwiches, and simple entrées like grilled salmon. It also serves fresh-squeezed lemonade in summer and hot apple cider in winter.

Bars & Nightlife:

Unpretentious **Silvertone Bar & Grill (56)** *(69 Bromfield St., 617-338-7887, www.silvertonedowntown.com, M–F 11:30AM–2AM, Sa 6PM–2AM)* is known for its reasonably priced drinks and tasty comfort food; their mac and cheese is just as you remember as a kid. The libations are potent at **Good Life (57)** *(28 Kingston St., 617-451-2622,* *www.goodlifebar.com, M–F 11:30AM–2AM, Sa 11AM–2AM, Su 11AM–10PM)*, where the emphasis is on its high-end frozen vodka bar. DJs spin house, hip-hop, and techno in its lower-level bar, **Afterlife**, most nights. Well-heeled urban sophisticates frequent **Kingston Station (58)** *(25 Kingston St., 617-482-6282, www.kingstonstation.com, Su 11AM–3PM, M–W 11:30AM–midnight, Th–F 11:30AM–2AM, Sa 5PM–2AM)* for live music on Friday and Saturday nights and a massive bar that features classy cocktails and a lengthy list of craft brews. Weeknights and at lunch, join the local office-worker crowd for high-end comfort cuisine like Vietnamese roasted chicken and vegetarian rigatoni.

WHERE TO SHOP

Pedestrian-only Downtown Crossing *(Washington, Winter, and Summer Sts.)* has more than 200 retailers, from major chains to specialty boutiques. This is the location of the legendary **Filene's Basement** *(426 Washington St., www.filenesbasement.com)*, dating from 1908. This was the chain's flagship store; it recently closed its doors forever—much to the dismay of long-time "bah-gain" shoppers. Though Filene's is no more, many long-standing local businesses remain. **Bromfield Pen Shop (59)** *(5 Bromfield St., 617-482-9053, http://bromfieldpenshop.com, M–F 8:30AM–5:30PM, Sa 10AM–5PM, open Su noon–5PM only between Thanksgiving and Christmas)* vends beautiful designer pens for those who value writing with flair. Its high-end styluses employ materials from wood to gold to resin and lacquer, as well as a few truly unusual substances, such as palladium. The shop also offers less-rarefied, but still attractive, pens at more modest prices. **Macy's (60)** *(450 Washington St., 617-*

357-3000, www.macys.com, M–Sa 10AM–9PM, Su 11AM–8PM) department store carries clothing, jewelry, shoes, housewares, and linens. Crafty folk have been coming to **Windsor Button (61)** *(35 Temple Pl., 617-482-4969, www.windsorbutton.com, M–W, F 10AM–6PM, Th 10AM–7PM, Sa 10AM–5:30PM)* since 1936 for—well—buttons (they're said to have the largest selection in the Northeast), plus sewing notions, yarns, patterns, scrapbooking supplies, and much more. Bibliophiles pilgrimage to **Brattle Book Shop (62)** *(9 West St., 617-542-0210, www.brattlebookshop. com, M–Sa 9AM–5:30PM)* for used, rare, and antiquarian books. Proprietor Ken Gloss often does book appraisals for *Antiques Roadshow*. The shop's alley bargain book area is a Boston institution. **Lannan Ship Model Gallery (63)** *(99 High St., 617-451-2650, www.lannangallery.com, M–F 10:30AM–4PM, Sa 12:30PM–4PM)* is the largest marine gallery in the world specializing in museum-quality ship models and nautical antiques. Students and bibliophiles while away weekend afternoons sifting the shelves at **Commonwealth Books (64)** *(9 Spring Lane, 617-338-6328, www.commonwealthbooks.com, M–Sa 10AM–7PM, Su 11AM–5PM)*, offering quality scholarly titles and antiquarian books, prints, and photographs; used paperbacks are downstairs. The shop is also home to independent poetry publisher **Black Widow Press**.

WHERE TO STAY

You can stay at the landmark **Custom House (43)** *(see page 39)*, now **Marriott's Custom House ($$$)** *(3 McKinley Sq., 617-310-6300, www.marriott.com)*, offering one-bedroom, one-bath suites with microwaves and refrigerators.

Opened in 1855, **Omni Parker House (65) ($$$)** *(60 School St., 617-227-8600, www.omnihotels.com)* is America's oldest continuously operating hotel. Guests have included Babe Ruth, Judy Garland, Ulysses S. Grant, Bill Clinton, and FDR. JFK announced his candidacy for U.S. Congress here, and proposed to Jacqueline Bouvier at Table 40 in **Parker's Restaurant ($$-$$$)** *(M–F 6:30AM–11AM, 11:30AM–2PM, Sa–Su 7AM–noon, M–Th 5:30PM–10PM, F–Sa 5PM–10PM)*. "Parker's" also played host to the 19th century's literary Saturday Club; members included Longfellow, Emerson, Hawthorne, and Dickens, who gave the first American reading of *A Christmas Carol* here. More history: Malcolm X bussed tables in the 1940s, Ho Chi Minh was a pastry chef, and Emeril Lagasse cooked here. The Parker House Roll and Boston Scrod were invented here. So was the Boston Cream Pie, official dessert of Massachusetts (it beat out the Toll House Cookie). Today's guests find accommodations combine heirloom-quality furnishings with modern amenities. The lobby and public areas are ornate yet comfortable, and the 500-plus historic rooms are gracious and quiet, but may be smaller than expected. Sample a slice of pie in the restaurant, or sip a signature martini in **The Last Hurrah bar**.

Around the corner, sleek neighbor **Nine Zero (66) ($$$)** *(90 Tremont St., 617-772-5800, www.ninezerohotel.com)* also boasts a great downtown location with a smart, modern vibe. Its Cloud Nine penthouse suite boasts floor-to-

chapter 2

GOVERNMENT CENTER

FANEUIL HALL MARKETPLACE

WEST END/NORTH STATION

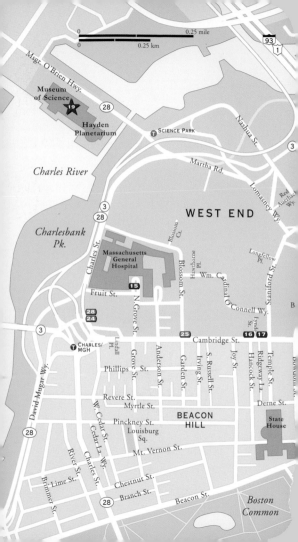

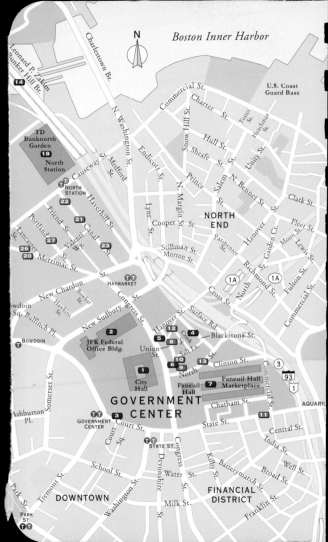

ceiling windows, viewing telescopes, plasma TVs, and Jacuzzis. A favorite guest amenity is a hosted evening wine hour. Note to pet owners: four-legged guests are welcome here with no restriction on type and size of pet. Upscale elegance is the hallmark of the **Langham Hotel (67) ($$$)** *(250 Franklin St., 617-451-1900, http://boston.langham hotels.com)*. The 1922 Renaissance Revival building was once Boston's Federal Reserve Bank. **Chuan Body + Soul** is the hotel's Asian–inspired spa facility, fitness center, and indoor lap pool. **Bond ($$$)** *(617-956-8765, www.bond restaurant.com, daily 11AM–2AM)* is shaking things up in the staid financial district, serving lunch, afternoon tea, and small-plate global cuisine and glam cocktails into the wee hours. Its **Café Fleuri ($$-$$$)** *(617-451-1900, M–F 6:30AM–2PM, Sa–Su 7AM–11AM)*, Saturday Chocolate Bar *(11AM–3PM)*, and Sunday jazz brunch *(11AM–3PM)* are popular with locals.

With handsome rooms done up in chocolate brown and taupe, the **Hyatt Regency Boston (68) ($$$)** *(1 Ave. de Lafayette, 617-912-1234, www.regencybostonhyatt.com)* proves even chain hotels can do urban-hotel chic. The hotel caters to business travelers, but an indoor pool and weekend specials make it a good choice for vacationing families. You might not expect great aesthetics from a downtown hotel with rooms that go for under $200 a night, but that's just what you get at **Harborside Inn (69) ($$)** *(185 State St., 617-723-7500, www.harborsideinn boston.com)*. The 98 rooms have been carved out of renovated 19th-century warehouse buildings; are all charmingly quirky and have recently been updated with a subtle nautical theme.

Places to See:

1. City Hall
2. John F. Kennedy Federal Office Building
3. Steaming Kettle
4. Haymarket
5. New England Holocaust Memorial
6. James Michael Curley Park
7. Faneuil Hall Marketplace & National Park Service Visitor Center
14. Leonard P. Zakim Bunker Hill Bridge
15. Massachusetts General Hospital
16. Harrison Gray Otis House
17. Old West Church
18. TD Garden
19. MUSEUM OF SCIENCE ★

Places to Eat & Drink:

7. Faneuil Hall Marketplace
   Durgin-Park
   Quincy Market
8. Union Oyster House
9. The Purple Shamrock
10. Hennessy's
11. The Black Rose
12. Green Dragon
20. Flat Iron Boston Restaurant, Tapas Bar, & Lounge
21. Boston Beer Works
22. The Fours
23. Grand Canal
24. Alibi

Where to Shop:

7. Faneuil Hall Marketplace
   Geoclassics
   Boston Pewter Company
   Bill Rodgers Running Center
19. Museum of Science
    Museum Store

Where to Stay:

13. Millennium Bostonian Hotel
25. Holiday Inn Boston at Beacon Hill
26. Bulfinch Hotel
27. Onyx Hotel
28. Liberty Hotel

★ *Top Pick*

Green and Blue Lines to Government Center Station
Blue and Orange Lines to State Street Station

• SNAPSHOT •

Boston is an architecturally rich city in the most traditional sense, and its citizenry has had a love/hate relationship with the concept of urban renewal. Today's drab Government Center, for example, was once Boston's bawdy Scollay Square. Lined with theaters, bars, tattoo parlors, and strip clubs catering to sailors on shore leave, the square teemed with "burlies and girlies." Its 1960s transformation into Government Center and its City Hall Plaza is generally considered to be an example of renewal run amok. And while most every world-class city now seems to have a colorful urban market center, Boston's Faneuil Hall Marketplace—with its historic buildings, cobblestones, flower market, street performers, and more than 100 shops and eateries—blazed the way back in the 1970s. Locals refer to the marketplace interchangeably as both "Faneuil Hall" and "Quincy Market," but there are actually four distinct buildings here: Faneuil Hall, Quincy Market, North Market, and South Market. Attracting throngs of tourists and locals daily, it's a great spot for people-watching.

PLACES TO SEE
Landmarks:

As you exit the Government Center T stop, you can't miss the imposing structure before you. This is Boston's **City Hall (1)** *(1 City Hall Plaza, 617-635-4000, www.city ofboston.gov, M–F 8:30AM–5:30PM)*; its controversial architectural style, sort of an inverted ziggurat, is described as Brutalist Modern. The **John F. Kennedy Federal Office Building (2)** *(15 New Sudbury St.)* opposite, with its twin towers, enjoys more respect—it was designed by Walter Gropius, founder of the Bauhaus modernist movement. Along Court

Street, you'll spot a giant, gilded **Steaming Kettle (3)** *(63-65 Court St.)* mounted on the side of the historic **Sears Crescent Building**. Cast in 1873, and originally put in place over a teashop, the 200-pound land-

mark now marks the site of a Starbucks. The building's boiler room supplies continuous steam. **Blackstone Street**, the city's oldest commercial street, is named after Boston's first settler, William Blaxton. Raucous fruit, flower, and veggie vendors of the gritty, open-air **Haymarket (4)** *(along Blackstone St.)* entertain unintimidated grocery shoppers every Friday and Saturday year-round. There are meat, fish, and cheese shops here, too. Steps from the Freedom Trail, the **New England Holocaust Memorial (5)** *(Carmen Park, Congress St., 617-457-8755, www.nehm.org)* is a striking reminder of the victims of the Holocaust. Visitors walk a black granite path beneath six illuminated 54-foot glass towers that symbolize six principal Nazi death camps. The towers are etched with 6 million numbers representing those who died. In grate-covered chambers below each tower, smoke rises from embers that spell out the names of each camp. Neighboring **James Michael Curley Park (6)** *(Union St. across from City Hall and Faneuil Hall)* has two bronze statues (one standing, one seated) of larger-than-life, four-time Boston mayor and one-time state governor James Michael Curley, aka "The Rascal King," "Boston's Robin Hood," and "The Purple Shamrock." Son of immigrants from County Galway, Ireland, the charis-matic Curley won the loyalty of the city's ethnic commu-nities and dominated city politics during the first half of the 20th century. He also served two terms in jail, includ-ing five months for mail fraud during his last mayoral term. His story is said to have inspired the character of Frank Skeffington in the novel and film *The Last Hurrah*.

Faneuil Hall, **Quincy Market**, **North Market**, and **South Market** buildings are known officially and collectively as **Faneuil Hall Marketplace & National Park Service Visitor Center (7)** *(bordered by Congress, North, Clinton, Commercial, and Chatham Sts., 617-523-1300, www.faneuilhallmarketplace.com, M–Sa 10AM–9PM, Su noon–6PM)*. Until the 1960s, the complex comprised the city's main wholesale food distribution center. Now, with its cobblestone promenade, pushcart merchants, street performers, shops, and restaurants, it's a magnet for visitors and, during the week, local workers. **Quincy Market** *(directly* *behind Faneuil Hall)* is the complex's centerpiece; the colonnaded granite Greek Revival building features a restored atrium that houses a popular food hall. The red brick **North** and **South Market** buildings *(on either side of Quincy Market)* were once warehouses; they're now filled with chain and independent shops and restaurants. Elegant **Faneuil Hall** *(North and Congress Sts., 617-242-5642, daily 9AM–5PM, historical talks by National Park Rangers every 30 minutes)* has been the site of political speechmaking since Revolutionary times. A gift to the city from merchant Peter Faneuil, the hall was established as a meeting place and marketplace. Here Samuel Adams, Daniel Webster, Jefferson Davis, and Susan B. Anthony rallied supporters for their causes. John F. Kennedy gave his final speech here  before winning the presidential election in 1960. The rooftop's charming 1742 gilded-copper **grasshopper weather vane** is original to the building. Boston silversmith Shem Drowne, America's first documented crafter of weather vanes, modeled it after the grasshopper of the London Royal Exchange. Faneuil Hall is also home to the National Park Service's state-of-the-art **Visitor Center** *(www.nps.gov/bost)*, which features all types of interactive bells and whistles, including iPad stations. It's the new starting point for the Park Service's popular (and free) ranger-led walking tours. Pick up a Freedom Trail souvenir at its bookstore and gift shop.

Arts & Entertainment:

For same-day, half-price tickets to theater, music, and dance performances all over town, swing by the **BosTix Booth** *(freestanding kiosk adjacent to Faneuil Hall, 617-262-8632, www.bostix.com, Tu–Sa 10AM–6PM, Su 11AM–4PM, closed M)*. You must buy in person. Both cash and credit cards are accepted. Event listings are posted daily; you can also check the BosTix Web site to see what's on.

Kids:

The kids will have a blast at the **Faneuil Hall Marketplace (7)** complex; its street jugglers, clowns, magicians, musicians, and mimes perform throughout the day.

PLACES TO EAT & DRINK
Where to Eat:

There are lots of mealtime options at **Faneuil Hall Marketplace (7)**, with many offering great regional flavor. Local bias aside, they are among your best food choices. Visitors and natives alike flock to **Durgin-Park ($$)** *(N. Market bldg., 617-227-2038, www.durgin-park.com, M–Sa 11:30AM–10PM, Su 11:30AM–9PM, bar daily until 1AM)* for authentic Yankee cooking, including cornbread, clam chowder, slow-baked Boston beans, and prime rib portions so big they nearly fall off the plate. Its famous sharp-tongued waitresses and long communal tables are part of the experience. Families on a budget and visitors on the go will find dozens of places to grab a bite at the **Quincy Market ($-$$)** food hall.

Choices range from Asian, Mexican, pizza, and seafood, to gelato, coffee, and cream puffs. The nearby **Union Oyster House (8) ($-$$)** *(41 Union St., 617-227-2750, www.unionoysterhouse.com, Su–Th 11AM–9:30PM, F–Sa 11AM–10PM, bar daily until midnight)* has loads of historic interest. With its uneven wooden floors and low ceilings, it is the country's oldest continuously operating restaurant, serving no-frills New England fare to locals, visitors, and notables since 1826. Historical tidbits: The toothpick was  first used in the U.S. here; John F. Kennedy often read the Sunday papers at booth 18 upstairs; and exiled Frenchman Louis-Philippe resided here before he became the last king to rule France in 1830. You'll find it a bit touristy, but where else can one slurp fresh oysters at the same semicircular bar where Daniel Webster downed his daily toddy?

Bars & Nightlife:

Irish bars with pints, live music, and tasty pub grub are a Boston tradition. Start your pub crawl across from **Faneuil Hall**. Tourists pile into **The Purple Shamrock (9)** *(1 Union St., 617-227-2060, www.irishconnection.com, daily 11AM–2AM)*, named for James Michael Curley *(see page 52)*. Nightly entertainment includes live music, DJs, and karaoke. The menu features Irish and New England favorites, burgers, pastas, and sandwiches. A couple of doors away, **Hennessy's (10)** *(25 Union St., 617-742-2121, www.somerspubs.com, daily 11AM–2AM)*

has more of a local feel; in fact, it's been voted "Best Boston Irish Pub" by the Improper Bostonian for years. Expect brogues, Celtic tunes, beef stew, and shepherd's pie. Congenial Irish barkeeps and waitstaff at **The Black Rose (11)** *(160 State St., 617-742-2286, www.blackroseboston. com, M–F 11AM–2AM, Sa–Su 9AM–2AM)* keep it real; this venerable pub has hosted musical acts from the Emerald Isle nightly for over 30 years, including the Chieftains, flutist James Galway, and a "once little-known lad from U2." Paul Revere and the Sons of Liberty favored the **Green Dragon (12)** *(11 Marshall St., 617-367-0055, www.somerspubs.com, daily 11AM–2AM)*, founded in 1657. This smaller pub attracts a sociable mix of after-five workers and tourists, serves imported beers, has live music Thursdays through Saturdays, and offers Irish Breakfast *(Sa 11AM–3PM)*.

WHERE TO SHOP

There are shops galore at **Faneuil Hall Marketplace (7)**, including national chains like Ann Taylor, Build-a-Bear Workshop, Coach, Crate & Barrel, and Orvis. Outlets with a local angle include the **Boston Museum of Fine Arts Shop**, a **Bostonian Society Museum Shop**, **Boston Campus Gear**, the **Yankee Candle Company**, and a **Cheers Gift Shop**. Be sure to poke around among the kiosks and pushcart vendors as well. Some of the most intriguing shopping comes from carts featuring ethnic items from around the world. Among the unique local merchants: **Geoclassics** *(N. Market bldg., 617-523-6112, www.geoclassics.com, M–Sa 10AM–9PM, Su noon–6PM)*, offering fossil and mineral specimens, gemstone jewelry, and items like Baltic amber Buddhas, tiger's-eye pill-boxes, and magnifying glasses with red jasper handles. Souvenir idea: A classic Revere Bowl from the **Boston Pewter Company** *(S. Market bldg., 617-523-1776, www.bostonpewtercompany.com, M–Sa 10AM–9PM, Su noon–6PM)*. The shop offers high-quality, hand-crafted pewter items, as well as scrimshaw, copper weather vanes, and more. **Bill Rodgers Running Center** *(N. Market bldg., 617-723-5612, www.billrodgers.com, M–Sa 10AM–8:30PM, Su noon–6PM)*, started by the legendary marathon man, strives to match runners with the correct shoe for their feet, regardless of brand or price. It also carries official Boston Marathon merchandise.

WHERE TO STAY

The newly remodeled **Millennium Bostonian Hotel (13)** (**$$$**) *(26 North St., 617-523-3600, www.millenniumhotels.com)*, right on the **Freedom Trail** *(see page 12)*, is in the center of all the action. Three 19th-century brick buildings combine to provide residential-style accommodations; some rooms offer working fireplaces or step-out balconies with French doors, flower boxes, and views of bustling **Faneuil Hall Marketplace (7)**. (Soundproofing assures you of a good night's sleep.)

"Solid men of Boston, make no long orations; Solid men of Boston, drink no long potations; Solid men of Boston, go to bed at sundown; Never lose your way like the loggerheads of London."

—*Author unknown*

Green Line to Science Park Station
Red Line to Charles/MGH Station

• SNAPSHOT •

Wedged between Beacon Hill and the North End, many call this district "North Station" after the area's busy transportation hub (which offers connections for the MBTA's T, commuter rail, buses, water taxis, and Amtrak's Maine *Downeaster*), but this is really Boston's West End. Once a neighborhood of narrow streets, shops, and tenements that served as home to Italian, Polish, and Jewish immigrant families, and blacksmiths, metal smiths, furniture makers, and millers of coffee and spices, the area was razed and families displaced 50 years ago in the name of urban renewal. Anchored by the TD Garden arena, the Museum of Science, and Massachusetts General Hospital, the area is a popular entertainment and family destination.

PLACES TO SEE
Landmarks:

The striking **Leonard P. Zakim Bunker Hill Bridge (14)** *(spanning the Charles River at North Station, www.leonardpzakimbunkerhillbridge.org)* has only graced the skyline since 2002, but it instantly became a city icon. Designed by Swiss architect Christian Menn, the

"Zakim" is the world's widest cable-stayed bridge. It commemorates the work of late local civil rights activist Lenny Zakim, known for building bridges between people of varying backgrounds, as well as the Battle of Bunker Hill. Illuminated dramatically at night, it seems to float in an iridescent, blue-white glow.

Sprawling **Massachusetts General Hospital (15)** *(55 Fruit St., 617-726-2000, www.massgeneral.org)* was founded in 1811. Its original building, now called the Bulfinch Pavilion, was designed by eminent local architect Charles Bulfinch. Visitors come from the world over to see the pavilion's skylight-illuminated **Ether Dome** *(4th fl., open daily 9AM–5PM when not in use for meetings, inquire at main lobby information desk)*, where anesthesia was first used on a patient in 1846. The Ether Dome also contains a statue of the god Apollo, a skeleton, and a mummy named "Padihershef," an 1823 gift from a Dutch merchant. Vestiges of old West End can be found at the **Harrison Gray Otis House (16)** *(141 Cambridge St., 617-994-5920, www.historicnewengland.org, W–Su 11AM–5PM)*, a 1796 home designed by Charles Bulfinch for his

friend and Boston's third mayor, Harrison Gray Otis. This delightful abode has been restored to its original splendor, showcasing colorful wallpapers, carpeting, and elegant furnishings. It's also the home of Historic New England, an organization dedicated to the preservation of dozens of privately owned historic properties throughout the region. Next door, the brick **Old West Church (17)** *(131 Cambridge St., 617-227-5088, www.oldwestchurch.org)* dates from 1806. Once a safe house on the Underground Railroad, the church is now home to a United Methodist congregation. The original congregation was founded in 1737; one of its first ministers, Jonathan Mayhew, an outspoken advocate of colonial union, is said to have coined the phrase, "No taxation without representation."

Arts & Entertainment:

Home to the Celtics (NBA), the Bruins (NHL), ice shows, the circus, and big-time entertainers, the **TD Garden (18)** *(100 Legends Way, 617-624-1000, www.tdgarden.com; box office 11AM–7PM daily)* was built to replace the 1928 Boston Garden. The state-of-the-art arena has had several name changes since its gala opening in 1995, but for Bostonians it remains forever the "Gah-din."

Kids:

At the ★**MUSEUM OF SCIENCE (19)** *(Science Park, 617-723-2500, www.mos.org, Sa–Th 9AM–5PM, open in summer until 7PM, open F 9AM–9PM)*, the young (and young at heart) will have so much fun, they won't realize they're learning. Little ones like the live animal presentations, newly updated dinosaur exhibit, and hands-on activities. 'Tweens and teens go for IMAX films and laser/music

TOP PICK!

shows at the **Mugar Omni Theater**. The museum also books blockbuster traveling exhibits, such as "Body Worlds" and "Harry Potter: The Exhibition." You can also witness 15-foot lightning bolts being produced by the world's largest air-insulated Van de Graaff generator in the **Theater of Electricity**, and see butterflies from New England and beyond in the tropical **Butterfly Garden**. After a $9 million overhaul in 2011 (including a $2 million projector), the **Hayden Planetarium** enthralls with daily star shows. The museum additionally offers the opportunity to view local skies for free from the **Gilliland Observatory** (museum parking garage roof, 617-589-0267, F 8:30PM–10PM, weather permitting).

PLACES TO EAT & DRINK
Where to Eat:

Serving savory small plates, inventive cocktails, wine, and beer in a "hip black-and-paprika" setting, the **Flat Iron Boston Restaurant, Tapas Bar, & Lounge (20) ($$)** (Bulfinch Hotel, 107 Merrimac St., 617-778-2900, www.flatironboston.com, daily 7AM–11AM, 4PM–11PM) is a delight. Try their collection of small plate tapas; the chef's empanada of the day and spicy ceviche are best washed down with a seriously yummy Mojito. If you feel most everything tastes better with a beer, don't miss **Boston Beer Works (21) ($)** (112 Canal St., 617-896-2337, www.beerworks.net, Su–Th 11:30AM–midnight, F–Sa 11:30AM–1AM), serving pub food with flair. This cavernous microbrewery features an outdoor patio, billiards tables, and, for sports fans, 15 TV screens. The menu ranges from mako shark skewers to a hummus plate, and includes everything in between: pizza, burgers, chicken, salads, and more. Beer selections include "Bambino Ale," "Bunker Hill Blueebeery Ale," and "Patriot Pilsner."

Bars & Nightlife:

Located directly across from the **TD Garden (18)**, **The Fours (22)** *(166 Canal St., 617-720-4455, www.thefours.com, daily 11AM–midnight)*, named "Number 1 Sports Bar in America" by *Sports Illustrated*, is classic—no gimmicks here. The testosterone-transfused ambience includes multiple TV screens, an extensive collection of sports memorabilia, and a menu featuring hand-cut charbroiled steak tips and award-winning Buffalo wings. A spacious Irish bar named after the waterway that connects Dublin to the Shannon River, **Grand Canal (23)** *(57 Canal St., 617-523-1112, www.thegrandcanalboston.com, daily 11AM–2AM)* combines turn-of-the-century surrounds (including a fireplace, a grandfather clock, and red Victorian-style wallpaper) with live rock bands, a dance floor, and a convivial crowd of locals and visitors. A seductive lounge is just what the neighborhood needed. Repurposed from the old "drunk tank" space of the Charles Street Jail, **Alibi (24)** at the **Liberty Hotel (28)**, *(215 Charles St., 857-241-1144, www.alibiboston.com, daily 5PM–2AM)* is a fun setting in which to enjoy skewers of shrimp with mango and lobster

pizza, accompanied by cocktails with names like "Dirty Harry" and "Cool Hand Cuke."

WHERE TO SHOP

Shop for gifts and educational items for your favorite budding scientist, as well as fun apparel, books, cool gadgets, and more at the popular **Museum Store** *(617-589-0320)* at the **Museum of Science (19)**.

WHERE TO STAY

Holiday Inn Boston at Beacon Hill (25) ($$) *(5 Blossom St., 617-742-7630, www.hisboston.com)*, catering to week-

day business clientele and family vacationers, offers contemporary amenities, excellent value, and (rare for Boston), an outdoor pool. The **Bulfinch Hotel (26) ($$)** *(107 Merrimac St., 617-624-0202, www.bulfinch hotel.com)* offers chic (though small) rooms in a renovated flatiron building. The wedge-shaped structure makes for interesting room layouts—"Nose Room Junior Suites" have exposure on three sides. Boutique **Onyx Hotel (27) ($$-$$$)** *(155 Portland St., 617-557-9955, www.onyxhotel.com)* offers sleek red, black, and taupe decor and a lush **Ruby Room ($-$$)** *(617-557-9950, www.rubyroomboston.com, M–F 7AM–10AM, 4PM–11PM, Sa 8AM–11AM, 4PM–11PM, Su 8AM–11AM)* bar and restaurant.

Adjacent to **Massachusetts General Hospital (15)**, the **Liberty Hotel (28) ($$$$)** *(215 Charles St., 617-224-4000, www.libertyhotel.com)* was once the notorious **Charles Street Jail**. This four-star hotel preserves features from the 1851 edifice in its public spaces, but guest rooms have a sophisticated, subtle New England feel—think mahogany, stainless steel, and colonial-style fabric designs with unusual color combinations. The hotel's stable of high-style bars and restaurants includes Lydia Shire–helmed **Scampo** *(617-536-2100, www.scampo boston.com, daily 11:30AM–2:30PM, M–W 5:30PM–10PM, Th–Sa 5:30PM–10PM, bar open daily 5:30PM–midnight)*, which delights with intriguing interpretations of rustic Italian cuisine. Start your meal with a nibble from the mozzarella bar.

"In New York they ask,
'How much money does he have?'
In Philadelphia they ask,
'Who were his parents?'
In Boston they ask,
'How much does he know?'"

—*Mark Twain*

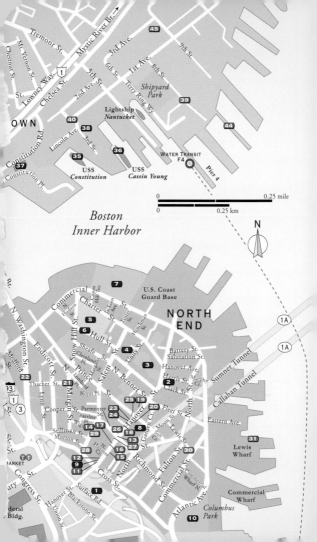

CHARLESTOWN

45

3rd Ave.

9th St.

Mystic River Br.

Tremont St.

Mt. Vernon St.

Chestnut St.

Lowney Way

Chelsea St.

St.

5th St.

6th St.

1st Ave.

8th St.

2nd Ave.

Terry Ring Wy.

Shipyard Park

39

40

38

Lightship Nantucket

Lincoln Ave.

3rd St.

44

35

36

WATER TRANSIT

F4

Constitution Rd.

37

USS *Constitution*

USS *Cassin Young*

Pier 4

Constitution Pl.

Boston Inner Harbor

0   0.25 mile

0   0.25 km

N

7

U.S. Coast Guard Base

1A

Commercial

Charter

Gipps Hill Ter.

Lindsen

Snow Hill St.

Hull St.

Jackson Ave.

Foster St.

Henchman St.

NORTH END

6

Sheafe St.

Cleveland

4

Battery St.

Salutation St.

3

Hanover Ave.

Harris St.

Salem St.

N. Bennet St.

Lombard

Murphy Ct.

N. Washington St.

Endicott St.

Prince St.

2

Clark St.

North St.

Sumner Tunnel

Medford St.

Thacher St.

Noyes Pl.

1A

22

21

Callahan Tunnel

93

Lynn St.

Cooper St.

N. Margin St.

Parmenter St.

25

19

20

Fleet St.

Eastern Ave.

3

Stillman St.

Bartlett Pl.

14

17

23

24

Hanover St.

26

8

18

13

Moon St.

Garden Ct.

Lewis St.

31

Morton St.

29

27

Lewis Wharf

MARKET

28

16

15

Richmond St.

Fulton St.

30

Commercial Wharf Ave.

12

9

11

North St.

Commercial Wharf

Cross St.

Atlantic Ave.

Congress St.

Hanover St.

Surface Rd.

Blackstone St.

Union St.

1

Columbus Park

10

Federal Bldg.

Commercial Wharf

chapter 3

NORTH END

CHARLESTOWN

NORTH END
CHARLESTOWN

Places to See:
1. North End Park
2. St. Stephen's Church
3. Paul Revere Mall
4. Old North Church
5. Copp's Hill Burying Ground
6. Skinny House
7. Langone Park
8. Paul Revere House
9. Improv Asylum
10. Christopher Columbus Park
32. Charlestown Bridge
33. City Square Park
34. Bunker Hill Monument
35. USS *Constitution*
36. USS *Cassin Young*
37. Navy Yard Visitor Center
38. USS *Constitution* Museum

Places to Eat & Drink:
11. Taranta
12. Lucca Restaurant
13. Gelateria
14. Antico Forno
15. Tresca
16. Marco
17. Modern Pastry
18. Galleria Umberto
19. Giacomo's
20. Daily Catch
21. Pizzeria Regina
22. Nebo
23. Stanza dei Sigari
24. Caffé Vittoria
25. Caffé dello Sport
26. Caffé Pompei
39. Style Café
40. Navy Yard Bistro and Wine Bar
41. Figs
42. Tangierino
43. Warren Tavern
44. Tavern on the Water

Where to Shop:
27. Salumeria Italiana
28. Acquire
29. Shake the Tree
30. Ball and Buck

Where to Stay:
31. Golden Slipper
45. Constitution Inn
46. Residence Inn Boston Harbor

Orange Line to Haymarket Station

• SNAPSHOT •

The Freedom Trail brings waves of visitors to the North End to see the home of Paul Revere, the neighborhood's most famous resident. They also come to see the Old North Church and Copp's Burying Ground. But it's the aromatic *ristorantes*, authentic *salumerías*, and tempting pastry shops that compel tourists to linger. Settled in 1630, the North End was a wealthy Tory enclave before the American Revolution. Over the years, the neighborhood was also home to African Americans and Irish and Jewish immigrants, though it's now largely Italian. As you wend your way through its picturesque streets, you might hear Frank Sinatra crooning from a café jukebox or residents cheering team *Italia* during a soccer match broadcast. Nearly every summer weekend, there is a *festa* to honor a patron saint. And Sunday morning Mass-goers greet each other with affable calls of *"Buon giorno!"*

PLACES TO SEE
Landmarks:

Tourists used to have to dodge Central Artery highway traffic to follow the Freedom Trail to the North End. No more, thanks to the Big Dig and the Rose Kennedy

Greenway, a park system created to replace the old elevated thoroughfare. Today, visitors traverse lovely **North End Park (1)** *(bet. Cross and Blackstone Sts.)*, a two-acre oasis of lawns, trees, and benches. The only surviving Charles Bulfinch–designed church in Boston is **St. Stephen's (2)** *(401 Hanover St.)*. Formerly a Unitarian church, it has been a Catholic parish since 1862. Rose Fitzgerald Kennedy, JFK's mother, was baptized here in 1890, and her funeral mass took place here in 1995.

As you stroll shady **Paul Revere Mall (3)** *(bet. Hanover and Unity Sts.)*, peruse the plaques mounted on its brick walls; they tell the stories of notable North Enders. The mall's focal point is sculptor Cyrus Edwin Dallin's commanding bronze statue of Paul Revere on horseback, memorializing the patriot's famous ride to Lexington to warn colonists that British troops were on the move. Legend has it the steed the silversmith himself called "a very good horse" was named "Brown Beauty." The mount was confiscated by a British

sergeant when Revere continued on to Concord. Must-do photo op: statue of Revere and "Brown Beauty" with loved ones in the foreground and **Old North Church (4)** *(193 Salem St., 617-523-6676, www.oldnorth.com, Jan–Feb Tu–Su 10AM–4PM, Mar–May daily 9AM–5PM, June–Oct daily 9AM–6PM, Nov–Dec daily 10AM–5PM)* steeple in the background.

Of "One if by Land and Two if by Sea" fame, the church, officially known as Christ Church, is where the predominantly Loyalist congregation's 23-year-old sexton, Robert Newman, hung two lanterns in the steeple on the evening of April 18, 1775, to signal that the British were advancing to Lexington and Concord by water. Built in 1723, the church is Boston's oldest and is now home to an Episcopalian congregation. Sexton Newman is buried in nearby **Copp's Hill Burying Ground (5)** *(bordered by Snow Hill, Charter, and Hull Sts., daily 9AM–5PM)*, along with "fire and brimstone" Puritan minister Cotton Mather; Prince Hall, the father of black freemasonry; Shem Drowne, crafter of the grasshopper weather vane on Faneuil Hall *(see page 53)*; and hundreds of African Americans *(in unmarked graves along the Snow Hill St. side)* who lived free here in a community they called "New Guinea." The burying ground is Boston's second oldest, dating from 1659.

Check out the **Skinny House (6)** *(44 Hull St.)* across the street—it's only 10 feet wide! Over two centuries old, the home is also called the "Spite House" because it was supposedly built to block a neighbor's view. Note: It's a private residence.

Take a break along the waterfront at **Langone Park (7)** *(along Commercial St., 617-635-4505, www.cityofboston.gov/parks, daily dawn-dusk)*. Watch the Italian gents playing bocce and enjoy the views of Charlestown's Navy Yard while the kids enjoy the playground. A small plaque at next-door **Puopolo Park** marks the site of the **Great Molasses Flood**. On January 15, 1919, a 50-foot tank containing over two million gallons of molasses exploded, sending waves of blackstrap through the neighborhood, leveling buildings, and killing 21 people. The molasses was used in rum and munitions manufacture; the explosion was blamed on various reasons, including anarchists, negligence, and a rise in temperature that day, which combined with molasses fermentation, causing tank pressure to build. Legend has it that on hot summer days, you can still smell the sweet.

Built in 1680, the **Paul Revere House (8)** *(19 North Square, 617-523-2338, www.paulreverehouse.org, daily Apr 15–Oct 31 9:30AM–5:15PM, Nov 1– Apr 14 9:30AM–4:15PM, closed major holidays and M Jan–Mar)* is downtown Boston's oldest building. Revere purchased the clapboard-sided Tudor-style house in 1770 and was living here when he made his famous "midnight ride." The house contains furnishings belonging to the Revere family. Tours are self-guided, but interpreters are on hand to answer questions. Across the courtyard, the 1711 **Pierce/Hichborn House** *(shown by guided tour only, call 617-523-2338 for daily schedule; combination ticket for both houses available)* was once owned by one of Revere's cousins and is one of the city's oldest brick structures.

The Freedom Trail
PAUL REVERE HOUSE

Arts & Entertainment:

Catering to 20- and 30-somethings (although patrons as young as 17 are welcome), **Improv Asylum (9)** *(216 Hanover St., 617-263-6887, www.improvasylum.com, box office Tu 2PM–9PM, W–Th noon–9PM, F–Sa noon–11PM, Su 2PM–9PM)* is wicked fun. Its improvisational and sketch comedy shows encourage lots of audience participation.

Kids:

On Saturday afternoons from May to October, the **Paul Revere House (8)** brings history to life in its courtyard,  with "Patriot" and "Loyalist" storytellers, period musicians, and demonstrations of silversmithing, leatherworking, and other crafts *(free with admission)*. Watch the boats sail by at **Christopher Columbus Park (10)** *(Atlantic Ave., 617-635-4505, www.cityofboston.gov/parks)*, overlooking Boston Harbor. This gateway to the North End is a perfect time-out spot for families, offering a playground, a wisteria-covered trellis walkway, and a rose garden. On sultry summer days, kids love nothing better than getting a quick spray from the park's push-button shower fountains. Note: **Langone Park (7)** offers a playground as well.

PLACES TO EAT & DRINK
Where to Eat:

Taranta (11) ($$) *(210 Hanover St., 617-720-0052, www. tarantarist.com, daily 5:30PM–10PM)*, named after Italy's tarantella folk song, features Italian cuisine with a

Peruvian twist. Intriguing menu choices include brined, double-cut pork chops with a sugarcane-rocoto pepper glaze, served with yucca *piatella* and a sauté of Giant Peruvian Corn, spinach, and caramelized onions. For dessert, you might try a "guavannoli"—guava and ricotta mini cannolis with pistachio brittle. Upscale yet unpretentious, **Lucca Restaurant (12) ($$$)** *(226 Hanover St., 617-742-9200, www.luccaboston.com, daily 5PM–1AM)* serves Northern Italian cuisine. Its dining rooms have a warm, romantic feeling, and floor-to-ceiling windows overlook bustling Hanover Street. Definitely make reservations. Obsessed with *gelato*? You'll love **Gelateria (13) ($)** *(272 Hanover St., 617-720-4243, www.gelateriacorp.com, daily 10AM–midnight)*, where fresh ingredients make for fantastic standard and seasonal flavors. Tourists mob **Mike's Pastry ($)** *(300 Hanover St., 617-742-3050, www.mikespastry.com, cash only; Su–Tu 8AM–10PM, W–Th 8AM–10:30PM, F–Sa 8AM–11:30PM)* for its famous cannolis. On a date or out with the family? **Antico Forno (14) ($$)** *(93 Salem St., 617-723-6733, www.anticoforno boston.com, Su–Th 11:30AM–10PM, F–Sa 11:30AM– 10:30PM)* means "old stove" and features well-priced oven-baked entrées, such as Pizza Margherita reminiscent of your trip to Italy and light-as-a-feather gnocchi. **Tresca (15) ($$$)** *(233 Hanover St., 617-742-8240, www.tresca northend.com, Su–W 5PM–midnight, Th–Sa 5PM– 12:30AM)*, owned by Boston Bruins hockey star Ray Bourque, is a stand-out among the neighborhood's high-end restaurants. The handsome dining space is large; the rack of lamb amazing. **Marco (16) ($$)** *(253 Hanover St., 617-742-1276, www.marcoboston.com, Tu–Th 5PM–10PM, F–Sa*

5PM–11PM, Su 4PM–9:30PM) has a second floor location, which is a little tricky to find. This tiny, chef-owned trattoria serves simple but sophisticated Italian cuisine. **Modern Pastry (17) ($)** *(257 Hanover St., 617-523-3783, www.modernpastry.com, Su–Th 8AM–10PM, F 8AM–11PM, Sa 8AM–midnight)* is the place for an espresso and an authentic Italian pastry. Crispy thin cannoli shells are filled with sweetened ricotta to order. Join the line at **Galleria Umberto (18) ($)** *(289 Hanover St., 617-227-5709, cash only; M–Sa 11AM–3PM)*, a lunch-only pizza joint that opens at 11AM. When the day's pizza is gone, it's gone. At **Giacomo's (19) ($$)** *(355 Hanover St., 617-523-9026, cash only; M–Th 5PM–10PM, F–Sa 5PM–10:30PM, Su 4PM–9PM)* you will likely wait for a table, but all will be forgiven once you tuck into the butternut squash ravioli in mascarpone cheese sauce. **Daily Catch (20) ($$)** *(323 Hanover St., 617-523-8567, www.dailycatch.com, cash only; daily 11AM–10PM)* has been packing 'em in (literally—there are just 20 seats) since 1973. As its name suggests, the *ristorante* specializes in seafood, often served right in the skillet. Try its lobster "Fra Diavolo"—fresh lobster, clams, mussels, shrimp, and calamari served over linguine pasta in a spicy, omega-red sauce. **Pizzeria Regina (21) ($)** *(11-1/2 Thacher St., 617-227-0765, www.pizzeria regina.com, M–Th 11AM–11:30PM, F–Sa 11:30AM–12:30AM, Su 11:30AM–11:30PM)* has

been making thin-crust, brick-oven pizzas since 1926, and they really are among the best in town.

Bars & Nightlife:

Enoteca-cum-restaurant **Nebo (22)** *(90 N. Washington St., 617-723-6326, www.neborestaurant.com, M–W 5PM–11PM, Th–Sa 5PM–2AM)* brings a touch of Milan to the North End. Share *quartinos* (small carafes) from an extensive wine list and nibble on mushroom- and mozzarella-stuffed *arancini* or grilled *salsicce* (sounds so much hipper than "rice balls" and "sausages"). Cigar aficionados enjoy their "draws" at **Stanza dei Sigari (23)** *(292 Hanover St., 617-227-0295, www.stanza deisigari.com, daily noon–1AM)*. The former speakeasy, in subterranean surrounds, oozes atmosphere, stocks premium cigars and spirits, and boasts a private cigar museum. The first Italian café in Boston, venerable **Caffé Vittoria (24)** *(290-296 Hanover St., 617-227-7606, www.vittoriacaffe.com, cash only; Su–Th 7AM–midnight, F–Sa 7AM–12:30AM)* opened in 1929 and is filled with vintage posters, photographs, and coffeemakers. It's a great spot for an after-dinner coffee, grappa, or dessert. Some swear by the tiramisu. At **Caffé dello Sport (25)** *(308 Hanover St., 617-523-5063, www.caffe dellosport.us, cash only; daily 6AM–midnight)*, the emphasis is on sports, especially Italy's Series "A" soccer league. Fans stay glued to its large-screen TV as they enjoy paninis, sweets, coffees, wine, or beer. Make the night last a little longer at **Caffé Pompei (26)** *(280 Hanover St., 617-227-1562, daily 9AM–4AM)*. Caffé Pompei is famously open late for Boston—until 4AM for cappuccinos, pastries, and Italian sodas.

WHERE TO SHOP

A Mediterranean grocery purveyor for more than 40 years, **Salumeria Italiana (27)** *(151 Richmond St., 617-523-8743, www.salumeriaitaliana.com, M–Sa 8AM–7PM,*

Su 10AM–4PM Memorial Day–Labor Day) is passionate about food and stocks high-quality staples—olive oil, pasta, coffee, and more. A bottle of their aged balsamic vinegar would make a great foodie souvenir. Both browsers and buyers are drawn to the bright gallery space that is **Acquire (28)** *(61 Salem St., 857-362-7380, www.acquireboutique.com, M 11AM–6PM, Tu–F 11AM–7PM, Sa 10AM–7PM, Su noon–5PM)* which sells antique and reproduction furniture and well-priced odds and ends like vintage seltzer bottles and hand-painted votives. **Shake the Tree (29)** *(67 Salem St., 617-742-0484, www.shakethetreeboston.com, M 11AM–6PM, Tu–Th 11AM–7PM, F 11AM–8PM, Sa 10AM–8PM, Su noon–6PM)* is a charming boutique featuring an eclectic mix of designer fashions, bags, mixed-media jewelry, fun gifts, home accents, and cute baby items. **Ball and Buck (30)** *(3 Lewis St., 617-742-1776, www.ballandbuck.com, M–Sa 11AM–8PM, Su noon–5PM)* refers to the musket ammunition commonly used during the Revolutionary War. Find classic menswear inspired by hunting culture, including jeans, khakis, and plaid shirts, along with fun gifts like Moonshine cologne. Nice, too, that everything sold here is 100% made-in-the-USA.

WHERE TO STAY

Seeking a unique hotel alternative? Stay in a classic 1960 Chris Craft cabin cruiser at the **Golden Slipper (31) ($$)** *(Lewis Wharf, 781-545-2845, www.bnbafloat.com, available May 1–Nov 15)*, a bed-and-breakfast afloat. The 40-foot vessel (which stays tied up) accommodates up to six and includes galley kitchen, living room, and bath.

CHARLESTOWN

*F4 Water Shuttle from Boston Long Wharf
to Charlestown Navy Yard Pier 4*

Orange or Green Line to North Station

• SNAPSHOT •

PLACES TO SEE

Sandwiched on a peninsula between
the Charles and Mystic rivers,
Charlestown, settled in 1629, was
originally a separate community
from Boston and the first capital of
the Massachusetts Bay Colony. Paul
Revere embarked on his famous ride

from here, and the Battle of Bunker Hill (really Breed's
Hill) took place here. The city was rebuilt after it was
razed by British cannon fire. Its famous Navy Yard shipbuilding complex was established in 1801, providing
work for scores of Irish immigrants who streamed into
the city decades later because of the Potato Famine *(see
page 39)*. Charlestown is still considered a bastion of
working-class Irish Americans, who call themselves
"Townies." The community was annexed by Boston in
1874. A century later, young professionals, attracted by
appealing colonial architecture, affordability, and prox-
imity to Boston, began snapping up its old row houses.
Now a neighborhood in transition, Charlestown boasts

a burgeoning dining scene, new and refurbished public spaces, and historically significant sights. Visitors arrive here via the Charlestown Bridge or the MBTA's F4 water shuttle from Long Wharf, Boston, to Pier 4, Charlestown Navy Yard.

Landmarks:

Freedom Trail followers walk the time-worn **Charlestown Bridge (32)** *(connecting N. Washington St. in Boston's North End with New Rutherford Ave., Charlestown)* to the sights across the river; also known as the North Washington Street Bridge, it dates to 1898. Once in Charlestown, pause to enjoy the flowers, fountain, and decorative sculptures of **City Square Park (33)** *(bordered by New Rutherford Ave., Main St., City Sq., and Chelsea St.)*, located on the site of the original 1629 Market Square. Stones in the lawn mark the location of the foundation for the Massachusetts Bay Colony's first public building: the Great House, presided over by Governor John Winthrop. The house later became Three Cranes Tavern, hence the bird weather vane on the central monument. The 221-foot granite obelisk northeast of the park is the **Bunker Hill Monument (34)** *(Monument Sq., 617-242-5641, www.nps.gov/bost/historyculture/bhm.htm, daily 9AM–5PM, no climbing after 4:30PM)*, commemorating the June 17, 1775, battle in which 1,500 poorly-equipped American colonists took a stand against 2,200 British troops.

The
Freedom
Trail

◀

BUNKER
HILL

The British prevailed, but at great loss; almost half their forces were counted as casualties (1,054), while the colonists lost between 400 and 600. The Americans thus proved themselves worthy, raising patriot confidence and causing a major setback for the throne. Fifty years later, 68-year-old Revolutionary hero Marquis de Lafayette laid the cornerstone for this monument, the first public obelisk erected in the United States. A 294-step climb to the top (there is no elevator) is rewarded by views of Boston, Charlestown, and Cambridge. The statue in front of the monument depicts Colonel William Prescott, who led the revolutionaries; generations of townie kids have stuck loaves of bread on his

outstretched sword. Across the street, in the former Charlestown Public Library, **Bunker Hill Museum** *(43 Monument Sq., 617-242-7275, www.nps.gov/bost, daily 9AM–5PM)* offers informative exhibits about the battle and the building of the Monument.

The main attraction of the **Charlestown Navy Yard** *(southeast of Bunker Hill along the waterfront)* is the **USS Constitution (35)** *(Pier 1, 617-242-5670, www.history. navy.mil/ussconstitution/index.html, Apr–Sep Tu–Su 10AM–6PM, Oct Tu–Su 10AM–4PM, Nov–Mar Th–Su 10AM– 4PM)*; launched in 1797, this is the

oldest commissioned warship afloat in the world. She was one of six original American warships authorized by the Naval Act of 1794 and was outfitted with copper bolts, spikes, and sheathing forged by Paul Revere. The frigate cruised the West Indies, sailed in the Barbary Wars, and saw lots of action during the War of 1812. Undefeated in dozens of battles, she earned the nickname "Old Ironsides" because cannonballs bounced off her thick oak hull. Active-duty sailors in 1813-vintage uniforms lead lively tours of the gun, top, and berth decks. Security is tight here; allow time for screening. The **USS *Cassin Young* (36)** *(Pier 1, 617-242-5653, www.nps.gov/bost/historyculture/usscassinyoung.htm, deck open summer 10AM–4PM daily, check Web site for hours the rest of the year)* is a World War II Fletcher-class Navy destroyer commissioned in 1943. Named for a Navy commander who won the Medal of Honor for his heroism during the attack on Pearl Harbor, she survived two separate hits by Japanese kamikaze pilots. For more naval history, stroll the **Navy Yard** itself; its dry docks, ropewalk, Commandant's House, Telephone Exchange, shops, and Shipyard Park offer a unique experience. Tours are offered by rangers from the Boston National Historical Park's new **Navy Yard Visitor Center (37)** *(Bldg. 5, 617-242-5601, www.nps.gov/bost, daily 9AM–5PM)*. The center also offers information on Charlestown, maps, and brochures.

Kids:

Furl a sail, fire a cannon, make a model ship, and learn about Barbary pirates at the **USS *Constitution* Museum (38)** *(Bldg. 22, Charlestown Navy Yard, 617-426-*

1812, www.ussconstitutionmuseum.org, Apr 1–Oct 31 daily 9AM–6PM, Nov 1–Mar 31 daily 10AM–5PM), offering hands-on fun for kids and maritime artifacts for history buffs.

PLACES TO EAT & DRINK
Where to Eat:

For a quick bite near the Navy Yard, try **Style Café (39) ($)** *(197 8th St., 617-241-7300, www.stylecafeonline.com, M–Sa 7AM–7PM, Su 8AM–6PM)* for egg-and-

cheese sandwiches at breakfast and top-notch sandwiches, salads, and smoothies in the afternoon. **Navy Yard Bistro and Wine Bar (40) ($$)** *(6th St., Charlestown Navy Yard, 617-242-0036, www.navyyardbistro.com, Su–Tu 5PM–9PM, W–Sa 5PM–10PM)* is one of Boston's best dining secrets, with a relaxed atmosphere and well-priced, well-executed

French bistro food with an international flair, like ginger-sake North Atlantic salmon with jasmine rice, seaweed and cucumber salad, wasabi crème fraîche, and ponzu sauce. Celebrity chef Todd English launched his restaurant empire from Charlestown way back in the 1980s. **Figs (41) ($-$$)**
(67 Main St., 617-242-2229, www.toddenglish.com) is English's upscale pizza restaurant, giving diners an affordable range of inventive thin-crust pizzas (the fig and prosciutto is gourmet pizza defined) and handmade pasta dishes like slow-braised short rib pappardelle.

Casbah-style decor, with red accents, low lighting, and canopy-draped velvet sofas, sets the stage for an evening to remember at sexy **Tangierino (42)** *(83 Main St., 617-242-6009, www.tangierino.com, Su–Th 5PM–10:30PM, F–Sa 5PM–11:30PM)*. The experience includes authentic Moroccan cuisine, belly dancers, and the downstairs lounge **Koullshi** *(open 5PM–1:30AM)* offers hookahs and cigars.

Bars & Nightlife:

Step back in time at historic **Warren Tavern (43)** *(2 Pleasant St., 617-241-8142, www.warrentavern.com, M–F and Su 11AM–1AM, Sa 10AM–1AM)*, known for its wooden beams, low ceilings, beers on tap, half-pound Angus burgers, and Curley's apple cake. Established in 1780, it was named for Dr. Joseph Warren, the Patriot leader who sent Paul Revere on his famous ride. George Washington once stopped here for refreshments. And Revere himself considered this one of his favorite watering holes; he led meetings of the King Solomon's Lodge of Masons here for 20 years. Patrons vie for outdoor patio seats at **Tavern on the Water (44)** *(1 8th St., Pier 6, 617-242-8040, www.tavernonthewater.com, Mar–Dec M–Th 11:30AM–9PM, F 11:30AM–10PM, Sa 10AM–10PM, Su 10AM–9PM)*, a great spot to sip a drink and enjoy the breeze on a summer evening. Its Sunday brunch *(10AM–2PM)* includes a make-your-own Bloody Mary bar.

chapter 4

THE WATERFRONT

SOUTH BOSTON
SEAPORT DISTRICT

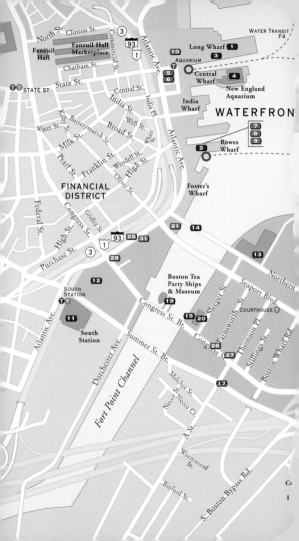

WHERE TO STAY

Located in the Navy Yard, steps from "Old Ironsides" *(see page 79)* and a ferry ride from Boston, the nonprofit Constitution Inn (45) ($) *(150 3rd Ave., 617-241-8400, www.constitutioninn.org)* offers deeply discounted rates for military customers, and welcomes civilians, too, with value-priced rates, comfortable accommodations, free Wi-Fi, and a fitness center and indoor pool. Your patronage supports the military. Located right on Tudor Wharf, all-suite Marriott's Residence Inn Boston Harbor (46) ($$-$$$) *(34-44 Charles River Ave., 617-242-9000, www.marriott.com)* offers waterfront views, a daily complimentary breakfast buffet, full kitchens, free Wi-Fi, a café, and a heated indoor pool.

"The place for an artist to live
is the North End."

—*H. P. Lovecraft*

THE WATERFRONT
SOUTH BOSTON
SEAPORT DISTRICT

Places to See:
1. Long Wharf
2. Rowes Wharf
3. Boston Harbor Cruises
4. New England Aquarium
11. South Station
12. Federal Reserve Bank Tower
13. John J. Moakley Courthouse
14. Old Northern Avenue
    Bridge
15. Hood Milk Bottle
16. INSTITUTE OF
    CONTEMPORARY ART ★
17. Fort Point Arts Community
    Gallery
18. Bank of America Pavilion
19. Boston Tea Party Ships and
    Museum
20. Children's Museum

Places to Eat & Drink:
5. Sel De La Terre
6. Legal Sea Foods
7. Meritage
8. Blues Barge
21. James Hook & Company
22. No Name Restaurant
23. Legal Harborside

24. LTK Test Kitchen
25. Miel Brasserie Provençale
26. Sportello/Drink
27. Lucky's Lounge
28. *Spirit of Boston*
29. Trade

Where to Shop:
4. New England Aquarium
   Gift Shop
11. South Station
    Serenade Chocolatier
    Barbara's Bestsellers
16. Institute of Contemporary
    Art
    ICA Store
20. Children's Museum
    Museum Shop
30. Louis Boston

Where to Stay:
9. Boston Harbor Hotel at
   Rowes Wharf
10. Marriott Long Wharf
31. InterContinental Boston
32. Westin Boston Waterfront
33. Seaport Hotel

★ *Top Pick*

THE WATERFRONT

Blue and Orange Lines to State Street Station
Blue Line to Aquarium Station

• SNAPSHOT •

Boston is steeped in maritime tradition, as both a busy trading port and shipbuilding center. Schooners laden with cargo came and went in the early 1800s; they were followed by packet boats and steamships. Within the last 100 years, however, the waterfront began to decline. Rotting wharves were lined with dilapidated structures; the harbor was polluted. A 1980s federally-mandated clean-up sparked shoreline revitalization, and in the last three decades, new and innovative commercial, residential, and open space development brought **★BOSTON HARBOR** back to life. Now colorful cruisers, graceful sailboats, and pleasure craft dot the water. And the city's unique HarborWalk affords pedestrians easy access to the sea front, as well as nearby parks, works of public art, eateries, water transportation, and more.

TOP PICK!

PLACES TO SEE
Landmarks:

Take in sweeping harbor views and watch the port in action from one of the many benches along **Long Wharf (1)** *(waterfront at State St. and Atlantic Ave.)*. Dating from the 1600s, the wharf was once the world's gateway to Boston. You'll find a covered shelter and a compass rose embedded in the pavement at the plaza at the wharf's end. The landmark **Rowes Wharf (2)** *(enter via the arch on Atlantic Ave. bet. E. India Row and Northern Ave.)* complex, with its yacht marina, stunning four-star hotel *(see page 90)*, shops, restaurants, and nightspots, makes for a memorable place to enjoy the color and activity of **Boston Harbor**. Take a seaside stroll here along **HarborWalk** *(look for signs at Rowes Wharf and along the water's edge, 617-482-1722, www.bostonharborwalk.com)*, a public walkway created by Boston Redevelopment Authority, Harborpark Advisory Committee, Boston Harbor Association, and property owners. The most popular section: between here and the North End *(see page 68)*. Now complete, the HarborWalk extends nearly 47 miles along Boston-area beaches, bridges, and piers.

Arts & Entertainment:

Cast off from terra firma! **Boston Harbor Cruises (3)** *(1 Long Wharf, 617-227-4321, www.bostonharborcruises.com)* offers whale-watching trips; sunset, sightseeing, and lighthouse harbor cruises; and fast ferry service to Provincetown on

Cape Cod. Its new turbo-charged *Codzilla* will whisk you out to sea on a wet, wild, 40-minute ride, music blaring. (Secure all hats, toupees, and comb-overs—no refunds for bad hair days.) **Boston's Best Cruises** *(providing service from various points of departure, 617-770-0040, www.bostonsbestcruises.com)* operates whale watch cruises in conjunction with the **New England Aquarium (4)** *(see below)*, as well as ferries to Harbor Island National Park area, and to Salem, Massachusetts.

Kids:

The four-story **Giant Ocean Tank** is the centerpiece attraction of the **New England Aquarium (4)** *(1 Central Wharf, 617-973-5200, www.neaq.org, Labor Day–June 30 M–F 9AM–5PM, Sa–Su 9AM–6PM, July 1–Labor Day Su–Th 9AM–6PM, F–Sa 9AM–7PM)*. Its man-made Caribbean coral reef is home to sharks, barracudas, moray eels, and schools of exotic fish. The sharks are awesome, but don't forget Myrtle the sea turtle; she really rules the tank! The **Marine Mammal Center** is a state-of-the-art exhibit that allows visitors to interact up close with fur seals and sea lions. Most recently, the aquarium opened its beautiful new shark and ray touch tank where visitors can reach out and pat a bonnethead shark or stroke a graceful cownose ray. You'll also find more than 60 penguins here, an outdoor exhibit featuring playful harbor seals, and a hands-on "Edge of the Sea" tidal pool for little ones, as well as information about the aquarium's renowned marine animal rescue team and ocean conservation efforts.

PLACES TO EAT & DRINK
Where to Eat:

You'll find two sure-bet, sit-down dining options right across from the aquarium. Award-winning **Sel De La Terre (5) ($$)** *(255 State St., 617-720-1300, www.seldelaterre.com, daily 11AM–10PM, W–Sa late-night menu 10PM–midnight)*, "salt of the earth," is like dining at a welcoming Provençal

country house. The menu combines south-of-France cuisine with fresh ingredients obtained from local farmers and fishermen. It's also known for its freshbaked breads, including sourdough, black olive, and fig and anise. Eat like a local at **Legal Sea Foods (6) ($$)** *(255 State St., 617-742-5300, www.legalseafoods.com, Su–Th 11AM–10PM, F–Sa 11AM–11PM)*. The family-owned restaurant chain got its start in the Greater Boston area; this is where native New Englanders go for great clam chowder, lobster, and fried fish. Bons vivants embrace **Meritage (7) ($$$)** *(Boston Harbor Hotel, 70 Rowes Wharf, 617-439-3995, www.meritagetherestaurant.com, Tu–Sa 5:30PM–10PM)*, an award-winning restaurant showcasing one of the world's largest wine lists—a 12,000-bottle collection of over 850 different varieties! Chef Daniel Bruce's menu of wine-friendly cuisine is refreshed each season.

Bars & Nightlife:

During the summer, the **Blues Barge (8)** *(anchored behind Boston Harbor Hotel, 70 Rowes Wharf, 617-439-7000)* is one of the hottest spots in the city. Its floating stage hosts live swing, soul, and blues music under the stars.

WHERE TO SHOP

Head to Faneuil Hall Marketplace *(see page 52)* for shopportunities near the waterfront. And don't forget to stop by the **New England Aquarium (4)** *(see page 88)* **Gift Shop** *(617-973-5266, M–F 10AM–5PM, Sa–Su 10AM–6PM)*, offering fun and educational items for all ages, including books, films, plush animals, apparel, and more. Proceeds support its mission to "present, promote, and protect the world of water."

WHERE TO STAY

The waterfront wow factor of the Boston Harbor Hotel at Rowes Wharf (9) ($$$$) *(70 Rowes Wharf, 617-439-7000, www.bhh.com)* is huge. Its signature arch and rotunda make a spectacular backdrop for the showy yachts moored here, the water taxis coming and going from Logan Airport, cruise ships, sailboats, and other craft. Rooms are the epitome of laid-back luxury. Enjoy the lobby collection of harbor maps and the views from ninth-floor **Foster's Rotunda**. It's all about the seaside setting at the Marriott Long Wharf (10) ($$$) *(296 State St., 617-227-0800, www.marriott.com)*. Its comfortable accommodations, indoor pool, and location next door to the **New England Aquarium (4)** *(see page 88)* make it a popular choice for families. The hotel also exhibits some harbor-related art and artifacts, including murals, paintings, and a 19th-century model of the USS *Constitution*.

SOUTH BOSTON SEAPORT DISTRICT

Red Line or Silver Line to South Station

• SNAPSHOT •

Boston's busy seaport is still the city's working port area, supporting fishing and cruise ship industries, cargo and container ship handling, and ship repair. But it's also become a real destination neighborhood. Described as "Boston's next great place," its Fort Point Channel district is lined with 19th-century brick warehouses that have been transformed into studios and loft spaces for New England's largest arts community—including painters, sculptors, jewelry makers, ceramicists, photographers, and textile artists. Star attractions like the sparkling Institute of Contemporary Art and the Children's Museum draw throngs of locals and visitors. Colorful galleries, eateries, and clubs add to the energy of this dynamic neighborhood.

PLACES TO SEE
Landmarks:

Dedicated with much fanfare on New Year's Eve, 1898, stately **South Station (11)** *(700 Atlantic Ave., www.south-station.net)* was at that time the largest railroad station in the world, and, for decades, the busiest in the U.S. Topped by an eagle with an eight-foot wingspan and a signature clock with a now rare, double three-legged mechanism (like that of Big Ben in London), the original Neoclassical-style building included a grand "Great Room" waiting area, mahogany and brass accents, gas lamps, an innovative Emergency Room, and a Woman's Room furnished with rocking chairs and cribs. By the 1960s, however, rail travel had declined, the New Haven Railroad was bankrupt, and the building had deteriorated. Boston Redevelopment Authority purchased the property but then began tearing it down. Outraged preservationists were able to list it with the National Register of Historic Sites, and demolition stopped. An award-winning restoration effort yielded today's bright, airy station, which provides connections for Amtrak, MBTA, buses, and taxis and offers dining, shopping, concerts, and exhibits. Need guidance for the bustling food court? Try **Cheeseboy** for gourmet grilled cheese sandwiches to go and **Rosie's Bakery** for cookies, bars, and cupcakes.

The distinctive **Federal Reserve Bank Tower (12)** *(600 Atlantic Ave.)* has been part of the waterfront skyline since 1974 and was one of the first harbor redevelopment projects. The tower floors were designed to appear suspended in air between two end cores. The natural anodized aluminum exterior is weatherproof, and the interior is shaded from the summer sun by aluminum "eyebrows," or spandrels; they also let in more light in winter. Located on Fan Pier, the curved glass and red-brick **John J. Moakley Courthouse (13)** *(1 Courthouse Way, 617-261-2440, www.moakleycourthouse.com, M–F 8AM–6PM)* is a highly acclaimed example of modern public architecture. The building offers tours, an art gallery, and dining options, too. **Old Northern Avenue Bridge (14)** *(spanning Fort Point Channel)* is one of the oldest operating swing bridges in the world. (Swing bridges allow boats through by rotating 90 degrees on a central pivot point.) Treat yourself at the humongous **Hood Milk Bottle (15) ($)** *(300 Congress St., Children's Wharf, open daily 10AM–6PM for lunch and ice cream during warm months)*. It's actually an ice cream stand featuring New England's Hood dairy products. The 40-foot wooden receptacle, situated in front of the **Children's Museum (20)** *(see page 95)*, has been a local landmark since 1977. It was originally built in 1934 and was one of America's first fast food restaurants.

Arts & Entertainment:

The stunning glass, wood, and opaque metal building on Boston Harbor is the home of the ★**INSTITUTE OF CONTEMPORARY ART**

TOP PICK!

(16) *(100 Northern Ave., 617-478-3100, www.icaboston.org, Tu, W, Sa, Su 10AM–5PM, Th–F 10AM–9PM, closed M except national holidays),*

founded in 1936. The museum is credited with introducing the work of artists like Georges Braque and Edvard Munch in the U.S. The ICA moved to this location in 2006; it's a unique setting for exhibitions of contemporary art in all media, along with its provocative permanent collection. The firm Diller Scofidio + Renfro designed the space in the shape of a folding translucent ribbon with cantilevered galleries, a theater, a plaza, and a "mediatheque" digital media center.

The **Fort Point Arts Community Gallery (17)** *(300 Summer St., M1, 617-423-4299, www.fortpointarts.org, M 9AM–3PM, Tu–F 9AM–9PM)* artist's cooperative is devoted to the work of local artists. Members sell art, jewelry, and more at **Made in Fort Point** *(12 Farnsworth St., 617-423-1100, M–F 11AM–6PM, Sa–Su 10AM–5PM)*. After dark, there isn't a lovelier concert setting than the open-air **Bank of America Pavilion (18)** *(290 Northern Ave., 617-728-1600, www.livenation.com; box office summer M–F and show days noon–5PM)*, presenting national and international musical acts during spring and summer. As we went to press, the newly expanded **Boston Tea Party Ships and Museum (19)** *(Fort Point Channel at Congress St. Bridge, www.bostonteapartyship.com)* was slated to reopen in summer 2012. Its living history programs and re-enactments tell the story of the events leading up to December 16, 1773. Explore replicas of three Tea Party tall ships—the *Brig Beaver*,

the *Dartmouth*, and the *Eleanor*, and enjoy your own tea party in the Sam Adams Tavern room.

Kids:

The interactive, innovative, and newly "green" **Children's Museum (20)** *(300 Congress St., 617-426-6500, www.bostonchildrensmuseum.org, daily 10AM–5PM, F 10AM–9PM)* is an awesome place for kids, from infants to ten-year-olds. The focus is on learning through play—by creating art with recyclables, investigating science through bubbles, exploring cultural connections at the Japanese House, and much more. Youngsters can't get enough of the 3-D, three-story lobby climbing sculpture-maze. (Mom and Dad follow on adjoining stairs that offer panoramic views.)

PLACES TO EAT & DRINK
Where to Eat:

Servicing restaurants and wholesalers around the country, **James Hook & Company (21) ($)** *(15 Northern Ave., 617-423-5500, www.jameshooklobster.com, M–Th 9AM–5PM, F 9AM–6PM, Sa 9AM–5PM, Su 9AM–2PM)*

ships more than 50,000 pounds of lobster a day! Sample some here at its retail showroom. We recommend indulging in the lobster roll—a hot dog bun piled high with chunks of meat. **No Name Restaurant (22) ($)** *(15 Fish Pier, 617-338-7539, www.nonamerestaurant.com, daily 10AM–10PM)* is

a no-frills New England fish house that's dished up fresh broiled and fried seafood to locals and tourists since 1917. Boston's exemplar of seafood restaurants, Legal Sea Foods, has a glitzy new flagship property, **Legal Harborside (23) ($$-$$$)** *(270 Northern Ave., 617-477-2900, www.legalseafoods.com; 1st floor dining Su–Th 11AM–10PM, F–Sa 11AM–11PM, 2nd floor dining Su 5:30 PM–9PM, M–Th 5:30PM–10PM, F–Sa 5:30PM–11PM, 3rd floor bar Su noon–10:30PM, M–Th 4PM–11PM, F 4PM–1AM, Sa noon–1AM)* with one of the city's finest waterfront views. The first floor features a casual all-day, mostly seafood menu. The second floor dining room is downright elegant with couples lingering over butter-poached lobster. Or drop in at the third floor bar and take in the waterfront scene. Across the street, Legal Sea Foods-owned **LTK Test Kitchen (24) ($$)** *(225 Northern Ave., 617-330-7430, www.ltkbarand kitchen.com, Su–W 11AM–1AM, Th–Sa 11AM–2AM)* combines high-tech ambience (with table iPod docking, Wi-Fi, and a changing mood-lighting system) with innovative multicultural cuisine. It has an extensive drink menu and zesty small-plate offerings—pizzettas, anyone? **Miel Brasserie Provençale (25) ($$-$$$)** *(InterContinental Boston Hotel, 510 Atlantic Ave., 617-217-5151, www.intercontinentalboston.com, daily 6:30AM–11PM)* emphasizes classic south-of-France flavors with items like tuna Niçoise: grilled tuna with sautéed Mediterranean vegetables, pan-fried potato, garlic, and Picholine dressing and bouillabaisse with lobster in a saffron-scented broth. **Sportello (26) ($$)** *(348 Congress St., 617-737-1234, www.sportelloboston.com, M–Th 7AM–10PM, F 7AM–11PM, Sa 10:30AM–11PM, Su 10:30AM–10PM)* is Chef Barbara Lynch's stylish Italian-style diner/trattoria, which features delectable bakery pastries and coffee for breakfast and bowlfuls of fresh homemade pastas like gnocchi with porcini mushrooms, peas and strozzapreti (literally "strangle the priest" in Italian) with braised rabbit, olives, and rosemary.

Bars & Nightlife:

There's no sign, but look for the red glow at the corner of

Congress and A Street, and you'll have located mildly divey basement bar **Lucky's Lounge (27)** *(355 Congress St., 617-357-LUCK, www.luckyslounge. com, M–Sa 11AM–2AM, Su 10AM– 2AM)*. The "Den of Cocktail Cool" delivers retro chill and serious cocktails—try its "Lady Luck" martini. Enjoy live music at its Sunday Sinatra Brunch. Dance in the moonlight during an evening harbor cruise on the *Spirit of Boston* **(28)** *(Seaport World Trade Ctr. Marine Terminal, 200 Seaport Blvd., Ste. 75, 866-310-2469, www.spiritof boston.com)*. It offers several cruise options year-round, including sunset, lobster, and dinner/dance cruises. Located downstairs from **Sportello (26)**, **Drink** *(348 Congress St., 617-695-1806, www.drinkfortpoint.com, daily 4PM–1AM)* is a clever concept—there is no drink "menu"; you tell the bartender what you feel like having and they will make a handcrafted cocktail using infusions of fresh herbs and specialty liqueurs just for you. Jody Adams has brought globally-inspired cuisine to the waterfront with casually sophisticated **Trade ($$-$$$) (29)** *(540 Atlantic Ave., 617-451-1234, www.trade-boston.com, M–Th 11:30AM–10PM, F 11:30AM–11PM, Sa 5:30PM–11PM, Su 5:30PM–9PM)*. Scan the menu for dishes like rosemary and ricotta salata flatbread, pomegranate-glazed eggplant with pine nuts, and whole roasted fish with lemongrass chutney.

WHERE TO SHOP

South Station (11) *(see page 92)* offers several shops, including locally-owned **Serenade Chocolatier** *(617-261-9941, www.serenadechocolatier.com, M–F 7AM–7:30PM, Sa 10AM–6PM)*, tempting you with Viennese-style truffles and dipped fruits, and **Barbara's Bestsellers** *(617-443-0060, www.barbarasbookstore.com, M–F 7AM–9PM, Sa–Su 11AM–7PM)*, stocking "all the books that fit." Discover unique design objects, jewelry, art books, and items for children at the **Institute of Contemporary Art (16)** *(see page 93)* **ICA Store** *(617-478-3104)*. The **Children's Museum (20)** *(see page 95)* **Museum Shop** *(617-426-6500, ext. 236)* offers fun and educational gifts. Having relocated to Fan Pier from Newbury Street, **Louis Boston (30)** *(60 Northern Ave., 617-262-6100, www.louisboston.com, M–W 11AM–6PM, Th–Sa 11AM–7PM, Su 11AM–5PM)* dresses Boston's A-listers and media types (both men and women) with designs from high-end established labels as well as up-and-comers. Its second-floor restaurant, **Sam's ($$-$$$)** *(617-295-0191, www.samsatlouis.com, M–Th*

chapter 5

CHINATOWN/LEATHER DISTRICT

THEATRE DISTRICT

11:30AM–10PM, F, Sa 11:30AM–11PM, Su 11AM–3PM, 5PM–9PM, bar open until 1AM M–Sa), is a fine choice for fashionable fare and a fabulous harbor view.

WHERE TO STAY

The contemporary, blue-glass **InterContinental Boston (31) ($$$)** *(510 Atlantic Ave., 617-747-1000, www.intercontinentalboston.com)* on the site of the Boston Tea Party has ultra-modern rooms that are spacious and baths that are well appointed. Imbibe a classic rum concoction at **RumBa Bar**, go for sushi, salsa, and tequila flights at **Sushi-Teq ($-$$)**, or catch a sea breeze on the hotel's two-acre promenade along Fort Point Channel. The **Westin Boston Waterfront (32) ($$$)** *(425 Summer St., 617-532-4600, www.westin.com/bostonwaterfront)*, connected to the Boston Convention Center, offers rooms with city skyline or harbor views and Westin's signature Heavenly Beds and Baths. Enjoy a drink at its urbane **Birch Bar** *(daily 11AM–midnight)*. Also convenient to the Boston Convention Center, the **Seaport Hotel (33) ($$$)** *(One Seaport Lane, 617-385-4000, www.seaportboston.com)* has more than 400 rooms and suites—including Allergy Friendly rooms—with triple-sheeted beds, coffee makers, terry robes, and harbor views; it also offers kids' amenities, a fitness center, a café, and **Aura ($$-$$$)** *(617-385-4300, M 6:30AM–10:30AM, 11:30AM–2PM, Tu–F 6:30AM–10:30AM, 11:30AM–2PM, 5:30PM–10PM, Sa 7AM–11:30AM, 5:30PM–10PM, Su 7AM–12:30PM)* restaurant and bar.

CHINATOWN/LEATHER DISTRICT THEATRE DISTRICT

Places to See:

1. Chinatown Gate
2. Chinatown Park
3. Chinese Folk Tales Mural
18. Piano Row Historic District
19. Massachusetts State Transportation Building
20. Bay Village
21. Colonial Theatre
22. Cutler Majestic Theatre
23. Wang Center for the Performing Arts
24. Schubert Theatre
25. Charles Playhouse
26. AMC Loews Boston Common 19

Places to Eat & Drink:

4. New Jumbo Seafood
5. Gourmet Dumpling House
6. King Fung Garden
7. Ginza Japanese Restaurant
8. Pho Pasteur
9. China Pearl
10. Les Zygomates
11. South Street Diner
12. Corner Pub of Chinatown
13. District
27. DaVinci
28. Mike & Patty's
29. Via Matta
30. Finale
31. Davio's Northern Italian Steakhouse
32. Jacob Wirth
33. Market by Jean Georges
34. Pigalle
35. Gypsy Bar
36. The Estate
37. The Royale
38. Sweetwater Café
39. The Tam
40. Jacque's Cabaret

Where to Shop:

14. Sun Sun
15. Eldo Cake House
16. Essex Corner
41. Showroom

Where to Stay:

17. Doubletree Hotel Boston
42. Boston Park Plaza Hotel & Towers
43. Radisson Hotel Boston
44. W Boston
45. Hostelling International-Boston

CHINATOWN/LEATHER DISTRICT

Orange Line or Silver Line to Chinatown Station
Red Line or Silver Line to South Station

• SNAPSHOT •

Boston is home to the country's fourth largest Chinatown, which today includes Japanese, Vietnamese, Korean, Thai, and Malaysian residents as well. Thriving in the shadow of mammoth New England Medical Center, this bustling neighborhood, with its pagoda phone booths and colorful storefronts, offers restaurants galore and unique shopping opportunities. Beach Street is the heart of Chinatown, and the primary destination for tourists, but check out Harrison Avenue, Tyler Street, and the alleys, too. Chinatown has the city's largest concentration of late-night eateries; when the bars shut down at 2AM, the clubbing crowd heads here. The up-and-coming Leather District, east of Chinatown, is the former center of the city's 19th-century shoe and leather goods industries. Urban pioneers were attracted here in the 1980s by lower real estate prices, industrial-chic loft living, and easy train station and harbor access. Hip restaurants and bars soon followed.

PLACES TO SEE
Landmarks:

Three-story, pagoda-style **Chinatown Gate (1)** *(Hudson and Beach Sts.)* marks the symbolic entrance to Chinatown. The red-and-gold gateway is guarded by a fierce duo of stone lions. Inviting new **Chinatown Park (2)** *(along Surface Rd.)* replaced an unsightly off-ramp left over from the old Central Artery. Combining traditional and contemporary elements of garden design, the park is lined with ginkgo, bamboo, willows, and other culturally significant plantings and serves as a gathering space for community events.

Arts & Entertainment:

Chinese Folk Tales Mural (3) *(Surface Rd. to the left of Chinatown Gate)* is one of four Chinatown murals painted by the Boston Youth Fund Mural Crew as part of an initiative to combat graffiti. There are two murals along Tyler Street: *Tale of 100 Children*, representing a traditional Chinese theme of luck, and a mural celebrating the neighborhood's YMCA. An antismoking mural dresses up a parking lot between Harrison Avenue and Tyler Street.

PLACES TO EAT & DRINK
Where to Eat:

It's fresh, fresh, fresh at **New Jumbo Seafood (4) ($$)** *(5-9 Hudson St., 617-542-2823, www.newjumboseafood restaurant.com, daily 11AM–2:30AM).*

The spicy salt calamari is always excellent and the sizzling seafood platter glistens with shrimp, scallops, and crisp vegetables. Don't let the line outside and the no-frills decor at **Gourmet Dumpling House (5) ($)** *(52 Beach St., 617-338-6223, daily 11AM–12:30AM)* dissuade you. This is the real deal for juicy soup buns and pan-fried dumplings of all types. Not sure what to order? Look at your neighbor's table and point! **King Fung Garden (6) ($)** *(74 Kneeland St., 617-357-5262, daily 11AM–11PM)* is famous for three-course Peking duck. Call a day in advance to order yours. **Ginza Japanese Restaurant (7) ($$)** *(16 Hudson St., 617-338-2261, Su 5PM–10:30PM, M–Th 11:30AM–2:30PM, 5PM–10:30PM, F 11:30AM–2:30PM, 5PM–3:30AM, Sa 11AM–3:30AM)* features super-fresh sushi prepared by skilled chefs and is one of the city's late night mainstays. A heaping bowl of pho (Vietnamese noodle, meat, and vegetable soup) is the way to go at longstanding Chinatown storefront **Pho Pasteur (8) ($)** *(682 Washington St., 617-482-7467, www.phopasteurboston.net, M–Sa 9AM–10:45PM, Su 8AM–10:45PM).* Love dim sum? Check out **China Pearl (9) ($)** *(9 Tyler St., 617-426-4338, daily 8:30AM–9PM).* This large, banquet-style restaurant packs 'em in for pillowy pork buns and tasty shrimp dumplings. Come early on weekends.

Located in the Leather District, low-key **Les Zygomates (10)** **($$)** *(129 South St., 617-542-5108, www.winebar.com, M–Th 11:30AM–10PM, F 11:30AM–11PM, Sa 5:30PM–11PM)*—the name is from the French and means "the facial muscles used to smile"—turns frowns upside down with its soulful bistro food, lengthy wine list, zinc bar, live jazz, weekly wine tastings, and three-course prix fixe menu. There are few 24-hour restaurants in Boston—**South Street Diner (11) ($)** *(look for the giant coffee cup sign at 178 Kneeland St., 617-350-0028, www.southstreetdiner.com)* is one of them. With an all-night breakfast and dinner menu, the 1950s-themed eatery is a favorite of sports teams, celebrities, musicians, and other night owls.

Bars & Nightlife:

The **Corner Pub of Chinatown (12)** *(162 Lincoln St., 617-542-7080, www.cornerpubboston.com, M–Sa 11:30AM–2AM, Su 5PM–2AM)* is an honest-to-goodness workingman's tavern with cheap drinks and decent bar food. The club-lounge-eatery, **District (13)** *(180 Lincoln St., 617-426-0180, www.districtboston.com, W–Sa 5PM–2AM)* is a little bit Miami, a little bit New York, with modish white leather banquettes and birch tree–lined walls. Try an "After Work Soother" or a "Boston Tea Party."

WHERE TO SHOP

Shopping in Chinatown can be an adventure. **Sun Sun (14)** *(18 Oxford St., 617-426-6494, www.sunsun boston.com, daily 9AM–7PM)* stocks oodles of hard-to-find noodles, soy and chili sauces, shrimp crackers, and

herbs alongside Asian cooking utensils and equipment. **Eldo Cake House (15)** *(36 Harrison Ave., 617-350-7977, daily 7AM–7PM)* sells delectable cakes, egg custard tarts, pork buns, bubble tea, and more, and provides a cozy place to sit. Its adjoining **Eldo Candy House** sells dried fruit and dried fish side-by-side with a kaleidoscope of intriguing candies in bulk. Sample white rabbit chews, chocolate stone candy, Gummi shrimp, and candied olives. Buddha statues, paper lanterns, and all manner of inexpensive toys and trinkets can be found at **Essex Corner (16)** *(50 Essex St., 617-338-8882, daily 10AM–7PM)*.

WHERE TO STAY

Doubletree Hotel Boston (17) ($$) *(821 Washington St., 617-956-7900, www.doubletree.com)* is a newer hotel offering modern decor based on feng shui principles, amenities that include Wi-Fi and access to the adjoining YMCA, which has an indoor pool. It's a very good value for downtown.

Green Line to Boylston Station

• SNAPSHOT •

Boston's Theatre District is one of the liveliest in the city
and home to more than a dozen
entertainment venues. On any
given night, it offers so many
performances, you'll be hard
pressed to choose among them!
Formerly seedy Park Square is
now restaurant central and offers lots of options for pre-
or post-show dining. The neighborhood is also home to
Emerson College, known for its arts and communica-
tions programs; the Piano Row Historic District, once
the nexus of the city's music industry; and Bay Village, an
enclave of homes dating from the early 1800s. The
Theatre District was also the birthplace of Edgar Allan
Poe, author of "midnight dreary" poem *The Raven*.
Today, striped shirts, socialites, and other (non-avian)
denizens of the night find a happening club scene here.

PLACES TO SEE
Landmarks:

Scores of prominent piano makers and music publishers
were located along the **Piano Row Historic District (18)**
(Boylston St. opposite Boston Common) during the 1800s
and early 1900s. The 1906 Beaux Arts **Steinert Hall** *(162*

Boylston St.) is said to be America's oldest music retail location. It houses the offices of piano dealer **M. Steinert & Sons** *(617-426-1900, www.msteinert.com, M–Th 9AM–6PM, F–Sa 9AM–5PM)* and four floors of showrooms, with more than 250 acoustic and digital pianos. The red brick building taking up an entire city block is the **Massachusetts State Transportation Building (19)** *(10 Park Plaza)*. Built in the 1980s, it's won awards for its energy efficiency and excellence in sustainable design. Inside you'll find an atrium, shops, a food court, and a small gallery. A plaque on Carver Street marks the site of the home (demolished in the 1960s) where writer **Edgar Allan Poe** was born in 1809. His parents were actors in a stock company performing in the area. The brick homes and cobblestones of **Bay Village (20)** *(bounded by Berkeley St., Stuart St., Charles St./Tremont St., Marginal Rd., and Cortes St.)* recall Beacon Hill; some of the carpenters and craftsmen who constructed the hill's fashionable domains built their own more diminutive versions here.

Arts & Entertainment:

The **Colonial Theatre (21)** *(106 Boylston St., 617-426-9366)* is the city's oldest continuously operating theater. Dating from 1900, this beautiful space launched a theater building boom in Boston. It's still a popular venue for Broadway productions. In the 1980s, Emerson College renovated Beaux Arts **Cutler Majestic Theatre (22)** *(219 Tremont St., 617-824-8000; box office M–Sa 10AM–6PM)*, the first theatre in the city to use electricity. Today, it's home to several arts organizations, including **Emerson Stage** *(617-824-8369, www.emerson.edu/emersonstage)*.

Magnificent **Wang Center for the Performing Arts (23)** *(270 Tremont St., 617-482-9393, www.citicenter.org, box office Tu–Sa noon–6PM)*, a Citigroup property, impresses with its grand staircase, 15-foot chandeliers, and gilded dome; dress up. It hosts big production shows, dance troupes such as Alvin Ailey and *Riverdance*. Across the street, exquisite **Schubert Theatre (24)** *(265 Tremont St., 617-482-9393, www.citicenter.org, box office Tu–Sa noon–6PM)*, nicknamed "Little Princess," is a venue for smaller, more intimate shows and visiting performers such as Aretha Franklin, Don Henley, and Steve Martin. The Schubert also serves as the main performance space for the **Boston Lyric Opera** *(617-542-4912, www.blo.org)* which stages four opera productions each year including a contemporary work, such as "Turn of the Screw." The **Charles Playhouse (25)** *(74 Warrenton St., 617-426-6912, box office M–Tu noon–6PM, W–Th noon–8:30PM, F noon–7:30PM, Sa 10AM–8:30PM, Su noon–8:30PM)* hosts two famous productions: Guinness Record–breaking (longest-running nonmusical play) **Shear Madness** *(Stage 2, 617-426-5225, www.shearmadness.com)*, a hilarious, hair-salon whodunit that encourages audience participation, and **Blue Man Group** *(Stage 1, 800-982-2787, www.blueman.com)*, with its wildly popular (especially with 'tweens and teens) off-beat combination of music, laser lights, and sometimes messy surprises.

If you'd like to catch a first-run flick while in town, the 19-screen **AMC Loews Boston Common 19 (26)** *(175 Tremont St., 617-423-5801, www.amctheatres.com, box office Su–W 10:30AM–11PM, Th–Sa 10:30AM–midnight)* offers state-of-

the-art surrounds and screens all the latest 3D films. It's mobbed on weekends.

PLACES TO EAT & DRINK
Where to Eat:

Dining preshow? Theatre District restaurants will get you in and out in less than an hour. Chef-owned **DaVinci (27) ($$)** *(162 Columbus Ave., 617-350-0007, www.davinciboston.com, M–W 5PM–10PM, Th–Sa 5PM–10:30PM)* charms with its artfully presented regional Italian specialties. In this neighborhood, a great breakfast/sandwich shop is a real find. **Mike & Patty's (28) ($)** *(12 Church St., 617-423-3447, www.mikeandpattys.com, W–F 7:30AM–3PM, Sa 8AM–2PM, Su 9AM–2PM)*. Try the "bacon and egg fancy" served all day, which consists of an egg cooked to order with cheddar cheese, avocado, and red onion on multigrain bread. **Via Matta (29) ($$$)** *(79 Park Plaza, 617-422-0008, www.viamattarestaurant.com, M–Th 11:30AM–midnight, F 11:30AM–1AM, Sa 5PM–1AM)* offers high-end Italian. Dine on the patio, downstairs in the kitchen, or upstairs in the sexy caffé bar or elegant dining room, where celebrity sightings are common. The focus at **Finale (30) ($$)** *(Boston Park Plaza Hotel & Towers, One Columbus Ave., 617-423-3184, www.finaledesserts.com, Su–M 11AM–11PM, Tu–Th 11AM–11:30PM, F–Sa 11AM–midnight)* is dessert (though lunch and a light dinner menu are served as well). Diners swoon over the "Magnanimous Molten" (best shared by two) and other artisanal sensations. At Park Square, 9,000-square-foot **Davio's Northern Italian Steakhouse (31) ($$$)** *(75 Arlington St., 617-357-4810, www.davios. com, M–Tu 11:30AM–3PM, 5PM–10PM, W–F 11:30AM–3PM, 5PM–11PM, Sa 5PM–11PM, Su 5PM–10PM)* includes an open kitchen, wine room, and take-out café *(10 St. James Galleria Atrium)*. The menu is equally as expansive, with fine cuts of meat, pasta, seafood, Italian specialties, a tasting menu, and much more. *Feinschmeckers* flock to historic **Jacob Wirth (32) ($$)** *(31-37 Stuart St., 617-338-8586, www.jacobwirth.com, Su–M 11:30AM–9PM, Tu–Th 11:30AM–10PM, F–Sa 11:30AM–1AM)* for hearty German and New England favorites and an international beer selection. Sing along with pianist Mel Stiller on Friday nights. Boxing legend John L. Sullivan once "suffered a rare knockdown" here while dining—he was struck by a beer barrel that rolled off a brewer's wagon into the restaurant. Boston's glitterati are drawn to **Market by Jean Georges (33) ($$)** *(W Hotel, 100 Stuart St., 617-310-6790, www.market byjgboston.com, M–Th 7AM–2:30AM, 5PM–10PM, F*

7AM–2:30PM, 5PM–11PM, Sa 8AM–2:30PM, 5PM–11PM, Su 8AM–2:30PM, 5PM–10PM) for seasonal cocktails and plates of Michelin-star chef Jean Georges Vongerichten's soy-glazed short ribs with apple jalapeño purée and rosemary crumbs, and crème fraiche cheesecake with passion fruit sorbet. Perfect for pre-theater dining, ooh-la-lovely **Pigalle (34) ($$-$$$)** *(75 Charles St., 617-423-4944, www.pigalleboston.com, Tu–F 5PM–10PM, Sa 5:30PM–10:30PM, Su 5PM–9:30PM)* presents classic French cuisine—cassoulet and crème brûlée—in a cozy, romantic setting.

Bars & Nightlife:

The red-velvet rope crowd has lots of choices here. Note:

Expect long lines, steep cover charges, and strict dress codes. **Gypsy Bar (35)** *(116 Boylston St., 617-482-7799, www.gypsybarboston.com, W 10PM–2AM, Th–Sa 5PM–2AM)* attracts 21-plus free spirits with its Wednesday international night and nonstop dance grooves on weekends. If dance clubs are your thing, **The Estate (36)** *(1 Boylston Pl., 617-351-7000, www.theestateboston.com, Th–Sa 10PM–2AM)* has a large dance floor and attracts a well-coiffed crowd. **The Royale (37)** *(279 Tremont St., 617-338-7699, www.royaleboston.com, F–Sa 10PM–2AM, check Web site for other nights)* is the city's most established nightclub with a large dance floor and an ever-changing line-up of DJ's and live bands.

Dine on the outdoor patio in warm weather at refreshingly casual **Sweetwater Café (38)** *(3 Boylston Pl., 617-351-2515, www.sweetwatercafeboston.com, daily 11:30AM–2AM)*, serving classic burgers, Reuben and grilled cheese sandwiches, pizzas, Tex-Mex, salads, and more. The café also hosts acoustic and trivia nights and has a DJ and dance floor. **The Tam (39)** *(222 Tremont St., 617-482-9182, cash only, M–W 8AM–1AM, Th–Sa 8AM–2AM, Su noon–1AM)* may be a little rough around the edges, but it's a welcoming spot to knock back a few with friends. **Jacque's Cabaret (40)** *(79 Broadway, 617-426-8902, www.jacquescabaret.com; cash only, M–Sa 11AM–midnight, Su noon–midnight)* gay bar and drag club is another popular spot. Upstairs, female impersonators entertain a fun-loving mixed crowd, including bachelorette partiers. **Jacque's Underground**, its downstairs club, features live alternative music on weekends.

WHERE TO SHOP

The **Showroom (41)** *(240 Stuart St., 617-482-4805, www.showroomboston.com, M–F 10AM–6PM, Sa 11AM–5PM)* is the source for contem-

porary furniture from Boston's top designers and also carries trendy European lines. There is not much shopping in the Theatre District; serious shoppers will want to head over a couple of blocks to the Back Bay *(see page 119)*.

WHERE TO STAY

With an on-premise travel agency, pharmacy, and ticket offices for Amtrak, airlines, and local entertainment, the grand, gilded lobby at palatial **Boston Park Plaza Hotel & Towers (42) ($$$)** *(50 Park Plaza at Arlington St., 617-426-2000, www.bostonparkplaza.com)* is always

bustling. Built in 1927, this is the city's largest historic hotel, comprising over 950 rooms, a sumptuous Imperial Ballroom, and top bars and restaurants, including M. J. O'Connor's Irish Pub, McCormick & Schmick's, and an outpost of the Melting Pot. It's said Liberace got his start in the lobby café. Well-appointed accommodations vary in size. At the conveniently located **Radisson Hotel Boston (43) ($$)** *(200 Stuart St., 617-482-1800, www.radisson.com/bostonma)*, rooms are—

well, roomy—and come with Sleep Number beds; many have private balconies with city views. **W Boston (44) ($$$)** *(100 Stuart St., 617-261-8700, www.starwoods.com/whotels)* has finally arrived in Boston. The hotel has a striking glass facade, super-stylish rooms, and high-speed everything. Relax with a cocktail in their trendy **W Lounge** *(M–Sa 3PM–1:30AM, Su 1PM–11:30PM)* located in the lobby. The latest addition to Boston's hotel scene is also one of the city's least expensive lodging alternatives. The 480-bed **Hostelling International-Boston (45) ($)** *(25 Stuart St., 617-536-9455, www.hinewengland.org)* is brand-new, with an eco-friendly design—including solar water heating, a roof garden, bike storage, and controlled lighting systems—and brings a new level of comfort and stylish accommodations to young and international visitors.

"In Boston serpents whistle at the cold."

—*Robert Lowell*

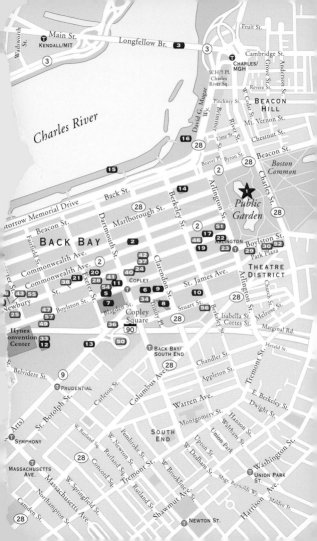

chapter 6

BACK BAY

FENWAY/KENMORE SQUARE

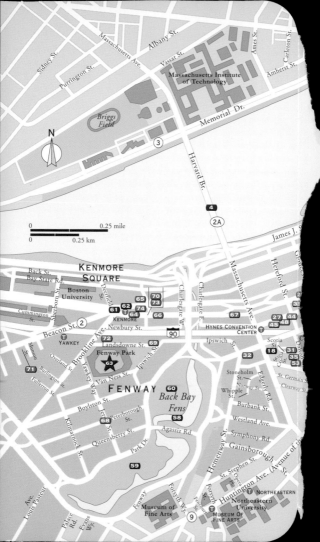

BACK BAY
FENWAY/KENMORE SQUARE

Places to See:

1. PUBLIC GARDEN ★
2. Commonwealth Avenue Mall
3. Longfellow Bridge
4. Harvard Bridge
5. Boston Marathon Finish Line
6. *Tortoise and Hare* Statues
7. Boston Public Library
8. John Hancock Tower
9. Trinity Church
10. Old John Hancock Building
11. New Old South Church
12. Prudential Tower
13. 111 Huntington
14. Gibson House Museum
15. Charles River Esplanade
16. Hatch Shell
17. Emmanuel Church
18. Berklee Performance Center
19. Robert Klein Gallery
20. Society of Arts and Crafts
21. International Poster Gallery
22. Barbara Krakow Gallery
58. Back Bay Fens
59. Kelleher Rose Garden
60. Fenway Victory Gardens
61. Kenmore Square
62. CITGO Sign
63. FENWAY PARK ★

Places to Eat & Drink:

23. Parish Café
24. Thai Basil
25. Café Jaffa
26. Casa Romero
27. Sonsie
28. Stephanie's on Newbury
29. Bistro du Midi
30. Bristol Lounge
31. Jasper White's Summer Shack
32. Crazy Dough's Pizza
33. Top of the Hub
35. Kings Lanes, Lounge, & Billiards
36. Minibar
64. Eastern Standard
65. UBurger
66. Petit Robert Bistro
67. Uni
68. Trattoria Toscana
69. House of Blues
70. The Hawthorne

★ *Top Pick*

"When they got to Boston, they felt too tired to fly any further. There was a nice pond in the Public Garden…."

—*Robert McCloskey,* Make Way for Ducklings

BACK BAY

*Green Line to Arlington, Copley, or
Hynes Convention Center Stations*

• SNAPSHOT •

Today the Back Bay may be one of the city's most exclusive neighborhoods, but until the 1800s it was just what its name implies—a back bay of stagnant tidal-pool water. The area was filled in as part of a massive late 1800s public works project that added 450 acres of land and utterly transformed the city's geography. Streets were laid out in a grid pattern. (It's one of the few Boston districts where visitors don't get lost.) Commonwealth Avenue is the Back Bay's grand boulevard. The one-way cross streets intersecting it were named alphabetically: Arlington, Berkeley, Clarendon, Dartmouth, Exeter, Fairfield, Gloucester, and Hereford. Although Back Bay is a showplace of Victorian architecture, some of the city's most modern skyscrapers are located here, too. It's also a premier shopping destination. ★NEWBURY STREET, simply "The Street" to those in the know, offers an eight-block retail paradise from Arlington Street to Massachusetts Avenue. Note: The renovated brownstones have shops at every level—basement, street, and atelier. Don't forget to look up and down.

TOP PICK!

PLACES TO SEE
Landmarks:

Lush weeping willow trees, regal Swan Boats gliding on a storybook lagoon, walking paths winding through prismatic flower beds . . . it's hard to believe Boston's ★**PUBLIC GARDEN (1)** *(bordered by Arlington, Beacon, Charles, and Boylston Sts., 617-635-4505, www.cityofboston.gov/parks)* was created out of landfill. While nearby Boston Common *(see page 29)*, a remnant of a colonial cow pasture, is dedicated to open spaces and active recreation, the **Public Garden** is decidedly Victorian formal and was America's first public botanical garden. Its centerpiece is a four-acre lagoon, which each summer is home to a pair of swans named "Romeo" and "Juliet." The darling footbridge crossing the narrowest part of the lagoon dates from 1867 and is thought to be the world's smallest suspension bridge. Unique to Boston: the lagoon's graceful fleet of **Swan Boats** *(617-522-1966, www.swanboats.com, Apr–June 20, 10AM–4PM, June 21–Labor Day 10AM–5PM, Labor Day–Sep 20 M–F noon–4PM, Sa–Su 10AM–4PM)*. They date to the 1870s, when shipbuilder Robert Paget received a boat-for-hire license for the lagoon. It's said Paget's idea of a pedal-powered boat in which the operator was hidden by a swan is based on the opera *Lohengrin*, in which the eponymous Grail knight crossed a river in a swan-drawn boat. Paget family

TOP PICK!

members still operate the attraction. Each boat (the oldest of which dates to 1918) takes 20 passengers on a leisurely, 15-minute figure-eight cruise around the lagoon; your swan is pedaled by a college kid who likely knows little of opera, but has very strong legs.

Influenced by the grand boulevards of Paris, tree-lined **Commonwealth Avenue Mall (2)** *(bet. Arlington St. and Charlesgate West)* is a nine-block greenway flanked by elegant brownstones. In April, pink-and-white magnolia trees put on a show. The mall begs a promenade; as you stroll, you'll encounter an assortment of bronze statuary, including sculptures of Viking explorer Leif Erikson, Domingo Sarmiento, president of Argentina, and a Boston Women's Memorial.

Two Back Bay bridges connect Boston to the city of Cambridge. The **Longfellow Bridge (3)** *(Cambridge and Charles Sts.)*, named after Henry Wadsworth Longfellow, is one of the city's busiest, providing daily passage across the Charles River for vehicles, the MBTA Red Line, pedestrians, and cyclists. Central granite towers give the bridge its nickname: "Salt and Pepper Bridge." It provides a great vantage point of the entire river basin. Further down river, the **Harvard Bridge (4)** *(at Massachusetts Ave.)* is the longest span across the

Charles. It is in fact much closer to the Massachusetts Institute of Technology than Harvard, and is known locally as the "MIT Bridge." "Smoot" marks are painted along the length of the bridge sidewalk; they're named for Oliver Smoot, a five-foot, seven-inch MIT freshman used as a human measure for a 1958 fraternity pledge.

Copley Square offers impressive landmarks. The **Boston Marathon Finish Line (5)** *(Boylston St. next to Boston Public Library)* is ephemeral—the word "finish" and the Boston Athletic Association logo are painted in blue and yellow a day or so before the race (which takes place the third Monday of every April) and fade before their repainting the following spring. Don't miss the whimsical bronze *Tortoise and Hare* **Statues (6)** *(Copley Square)*, a marathon tribute by local artist Nancy Schön. The Italian Renaissance Revival-style **Boston Public Library (7)** *(700 Boylston St., 617-536-5400, www.bpl.org, M–Th 9AM–9PM, F–Sa 9AM–5PM, Su 1PM–5PM)* was designed by Charles McKim in the mid 1800s. Bates Hall, the central reading room, with its barrel-arched ceiling, is

magnificent. The library features murals by John Singer Sargent and a set of bronze doors by sculptor Daniel Chester French. Explore the art and architecture on your own or take a library-guided tour *(offered once daily, see Web site for times)*. The sleek, blue-glass, I. M. Pei–designed **John Hancock Tower (8)** *(200 Clarendon St.)* is Boston's tallest building. Completed in 1976, it reflects **Trinity Church (9)** *(206 Clarendon St., 617-536-0944, www. trinitychurchboston.org, M, Tu, Th, F 11AM–5PM, W 11AM–6PM, Sa 9AM–4:30PM)*, the 1877 masterwork of architect H. H. Richardson. Inside, John La Farge's opalescent stained glass windows are particularly beautiful. The **Old John Hancock Building (10)** *(200 Berkeley St.)* is topped by a weather beacon; locals know the little poem that decodes the signals: "Steady blue, clear view. Flashing blue, clouds due. Steady red, rain ahead. Flashing red, snow instead." (Unless it's baseball season, then flashing red means the game at Fenway is canceled!) The 1875 Italian Gothic basilica next to the Copley T station is the **New Old South Church (11)** *(645 Boylston St., 617-536-1970, www.oldsouth.org)*, aka "Church at the Finish Line of the Boston Marathon." Its name includes the word "new" because the congregation's ancestral church is the Old South Meeting House on Washington Street *(see page 41)*. All of which goes to show that "old" in Boston is very old, and "new" is sometimes not really so new. The other big skyscraper in the neighborhood is the **Prudential Tower (12)** *(800 Boylston St., 617-236-3100, www.prudentialcenter.com)*, built in the early 1960s; it's a bit shorter than its rival, the **John Hancock Tower (8)**. Built in 2002, the Gothamesque cylindrical glass facade of **111 Huntington (13)** *(111 Huntington Ave.)* is a distinctive addition to the Boston skyline.

Arts & Entertainment:

Imagine how the other half once lived at the **Gibson House**  **Museum (14)** *(137 Beacon St., 617-267-6338, www.thegibsonhouse.org; guided tours offered W–Su at 1PM, 2PM, and 3PM)*, the restored home of a well-to-do Victorian family. Very *Downton Abbey*. The **Charles River Esplanade (15)** is a lovely three-mile ribbon of green parkland along the river. There are walkways, bike paths, stone footbridges, ball fields, playgrounds, and plenty of benches for taking in the sailboats and sculling crews on the water. The **Hatch Shell (16)** *(off James J. Storrow Dr.)* was built in 1941 and is an outdoor performance space for concerts and events from spring through fall. It is best known as the site of the nationally televised Boston Pops Independence Day concert *(see page 20)*. The giant abstract bust of fabled conductor **Arthur Fiedler** (he made the Boston Pops the most famous orchestra in the world and initiated the tradition of free esplanade concerts here) is made of layered, sand-blasted aluminum plates. (Who said Boston is staid?) The 1860 Gothic Episcopal **Emmanuel Church (17)** *(15 Newbury St., 617-536-3355, www.emmanuel-boston.org)* has a strong classical music tradition. Its Emmanuel Music orchestra and chorus, founded in 1970, perform a Bach cantata during its 10AM liturgy each Sunday from September through April.

The kids in black T-shirts hanging out around "Mass. Ave." are Berklee students. Of late, Berklee College of Music, the country's largest independent school for contemporary and jazz music is enjoying a high profile. **Berklee Performance Center (18)** *(136 Massachusetts Ave., 617-747-2261, www.berkleebpc.com, box office M–Sa 10AM–6PM and 2 hrs. before show-time)* functions practically as the school's laboratory, but it also books national and international folk, jazz, and rock acts. Art Garfunkel, Dave Brubeck Quartet, Joan Armatrading, and Chris Botti have been recent performers here.

Newbury Street is dense with prestigious galleries. The **Robert Klein Gallery (19)** *(38 Newbury St., 4th floor, 617-267-7997, www.robertkleingallery.com, Tu–F 10AM–5:30PM, Sa 11AM–5PM)*, specializing in 19th- and 20th-century fine arts photography by masters such as Eadweard Muybridge, Ansel Adams, Man Ray, Alfred Stieglitz, and many more. The gallery also hosts exhibitions that intro-duce newer photographers to the public. The **Society of Arts and Crafts (20)** *(175 Newbury St., 617-266-1810, www.societyofcrafts.org, Tu–Sa 10AM–6PM, closed Su and M)* has a second-floor gallery showcasing one-of-a-kind and limited-edition decorative art pieces. Incorporated in 1897, society founders developed standards of excel-lence in design and technical mastery for crafts that inspired the American Arts and Crafts Movement.

Purchase vintage posters from $50 and up at the **International Poster Gallery (21)** *(205 Newbury St., 617-375-0076, www.internationalposter.com, M–Sa 10AM–6PM, Su noon–6PM)*. The **Barbara Krakow Gallery (22)** *(10 Newbury St., 617-262-4490, www.barbarakrakowgallery.com, Tu–Sa 10AM–5:30PM)* is one of Boston's most established and important contemporary art galleries, displaying painting, photography, drawings, and prints.

Visit the sky-high, 50th-floor **Skywalk Observatory** at the **Prudential Tower (12)** *(Prudential Center, 800 Boylston St., 617-859-0648, www.prudentialcenter.com, open daily Nov–Mar 10AM–8PM, Apr–Oct 10AM–10PM, but sometimes reserved for private functions—call before you go)*, offering 360-degree panoramic views of Boston and well beyond, even Cape Cod beaches. An accompanying audio tour relates cultural and historic tidbits. Purchase tickets at the Skywalk Observatory Kiosk *(Prudential Arcade)* or at the observatory entrance.

Kids:

Generations of readers are familiar with the **Public Garden (1)** as the setting for *Make Way for Ducklings*, Robert McCloskey's 1941 picture book. Waddle after the kids to peruse sculptor Nancy Schön's irresistible interpretation

of the Caldecott Award-winning classic: bronze ***Make Way for Ducklings* Statues** *(near park entrance at Charles and Beacon Sts.)*. Mrs. Mallard is depicted leading her brood (Jack, Kack, Lack, Mack, Nack, Ouack,

Pack, and Quack) to the lagoon. Children hug, kiss, and clamber about the sculptures—it makes for a great family photo op.

PLACES TO EAT & DRINK
Where to Eat:

Designer sandwiches and wraps by Boston celeb chefs are a delight at **Parish Café (23) ($)** *(361 Boylston St., 617-247-4777, www.parishcafe.com, M–Sa 11:30AM–2AM, Su noon–2AM)*.  In fine weather, its outside patio is the place to be. The well-stocked bar is open until 2AM. **Thai Basil (24) ($)** *(132 Newbury St., 617-578-0089, www.thaibasilboston.com, M–F 11AM–10PM, Sa noon–10:30PM, Su noon–9:30PM)* hits the spot with spicy specialties like chicken coconut soup with galangal, lime juice, and hot chilies. Serving kebabs, falafel, hummus, burgers, and more, **Café Jaffa (25) ($)** *(48 Gloucester St., 617-536-0230, www.cafejaffa.net, M–Th 11AM–10:30PM, F–Sa 11AM–11PM, Su noon–10PM)* offers a fast, flavorful bargain bite in this high-priced part of town. Its robust Turkish coffee will fuel your shopping. The entrance is in an alley, but finding **Casa Romero (26) ($$)** *(30 Gloucester St., 617-536-4341, www.casaromero. com, Su–Th 5PM–10PM, F–Sa 5PM–11PM)*, decorated in vibrant Talavera tiles, is like discovering a hidden jewel. Authentic, upscale Mexican cuisine and fine sangria make for a memorable dining experience. In the summer, dine on the romantic outdoor patio. Try the signature pork marinated in oranges and smoked chipotle peppers.

See and be part of the scene at **Sonsie (27) ($$)** *(327 Newbury St., 617-351-2500, www.sonsieboston.com, daily 7AM–1AM)*, a magnet for the international crowd. Enjoy its downstairs wine room or dine alfresco in the summer. Wear black and don't forget the sunglasses. **Stephanie's on Newbury (28) ($$)** *(190 Newbury St., 617-236-0990, www.stephaniesonnewbury.com, M–F 11:30AM–11PM, Sa 11AM–11PM, Su 10AM–10PM)* has it all. In warm weather, it is a primo people-watching spot, with one of the largest outdoor patios in the city. Executive chef/owner Stephanie Sidell's menu leans toward sophisticated comfort food she calls "love food." Her lobster pot pie is a creamy, sage crust-topped blend of lobster, corn, pearl onions, peas, potatoes, and carrots. Dessert? How about old-fashioned peach and blueberry cobbler with vanilla ice cream? It's hard to return to the real world after experiencing **Bistro du Midi (29) ($$–$$$)** *(272 Boylston St., 617-426-7878, www.bistrodumidi.com, daily 11:30AM–10PM)*, where everything clicks from the luminous dining room overlooking the Public Garden to the inventive Provençal menu to the flawless service. The chef's five- and seven-course tasting menus are worthy of a splurge. Despite their famous (or perhaps to the British, infamous) Tea Party protest, Bostonians do love a proper English tea. **Bristol Lounge (30) ($$–$$$)** *(Four Seasons Hotel, 200 Boylston St., 617-351-2037, www.fourseasons.com/boston/dining, Su 7AM–10:30PM, M–Th 6:30AM–10:30PM, F 6:30AM–11:30PM, Sa 7AM–11:30PM)* serves a most civilized high tea every weekend, complete with scones, clotted cream, and oh-so-dainty sandwiches. "Boston's living room" is the main dining space for the hotel and also provides views of the Public Garden and, in winter, a crackling fireplace. On Saturday evenings, its dessert buffet tempts with cakes, crepes, and other confections.

Kids:

Corn dogs are one of the most popular items on the extensive kids' menu at **Jasper White's Summer Shack (31) ($$)** *(50 Dalton St., 617-867-9955, www.summer shackrestaurant.com, Apr–Sep Su–Th 11:30AM–10PM, F–Sa 11:30AM–11PM, Oct–Mar M–Th 4PM–10PM, F 4PM–11PM, Sa 11:30AM–11PM, Su 11:30AM–10PM)*, serving seafood in a fun, casual Cape Cod atmosphere. Its New England Clambake comes with all the trimmings. **Crazy Dough's Pizza (32) ($)** *(1124 Boylston St., 617-266-5656, www.crazydoughs.com, M–Th 11AM–11PM, F 11AM–2AM, Sa noon–2AM, Su noon–10PM)* specializes in unique topping combinations, artfully presented. For Mom and Dad: award-winning "Nutty Tuscan" pie with oven-roasted plum tomato, caramelized onion, garlic, toasted pine nuts, gorgonzola, fresh basil, and pesto. For the kids: just-right cheese or pepperoni.

Bars & Nightlife:

The **Top of the Hub (33)** *(800 Boylston St., 617-536-1775, www.topofthehub.net, M–Sa 11:30AM–1AM, Su 11AM–1AM)*, atop the **Prudential Tower (12)**, ranks as one of Boston's most romantic evening experiences. The 52nd-floor views are stellar, the drinks glam, and jazz smooth. Clubby **Oak Bar** at the Fairmont Copley Plaza *(see page 134) (138 St. James Ave., 617-267-5300, www.theoakroom.com, Su–Th 11AM–*

11PM, F–Sa 11AM–1AM), with its warm wood paneling, marble bar, and coffered, gilded ceiling, oozes wealth. This is also one of the city's best bars; its classic martinis were great here way before they were fashionable everywhere else. Make a night of it at **Kings Lanes, Lounge, & Billiards (35)** *(50 Dalton St., 617-266-2695, www.kingsbackbay.com, M 5PM–2AM, Tu–Su 11:30AM–2AM)*, across the street from the "Pru." This 25,000 square-foot, retro-style nightspot, a favorite with local celebs, features 16 ten-pin bowling lanes, eight billiards tables, 30+ big-screen high-definition TVs and projection screens, multiple bars, and a restaurant. Boston does sexy upscale lounge at **Minibar (36)** *(Copley Square Hotel, 51 Huntington Ave., 617-424-8400, www. minibarboston.com, Su–W 5PM–1AM, Th–Sa 5PM–2AM)*, the place for designer drinks and stylish small plates.

WHERE TO SHOP

Newbury Street is the place to shop in Boston. Note that stores closer to the **Public Garden (1)** tend to be more high-end couture. As you make your way toward Massachusetts Avenue, retailers are more diverse and a bit less expensive. Moneyed folk start at salons at the top of "The Street," such as Valentino, Cartier, and Zegna. Working your way down the street, **Fresh (37)** *(121 Newbury St., 617-421-1212, www.fresh.com, M–Sa 10AM–7PM, Su noon–6PM)* is the Boston-based European–styled beauty apothecary chain that makes it so easy to indulge yourself. Equipped with the right tools from **Kitchenwares by Blackstones (38)** *(215 Newbury St., 857-366-4237, www.kitchenwares boston.com, M–F 10AM–7PM, Sa 10AM–6PM, Su noon–5PM)*, you, too, can cook like a master chef.

There's also a full calendar of classes, tastings, demos, and author appearances worth checking out. The signature store of Boston-based **Britt Ryan (39)** *(291 Newbury St., 857-284-7196, www.brittryan.com, M–F 11AM–7PM, Sa 11AM–6PM, Su 11AM–5PM)* is filled with the brightly colored casual wear and chic dress styles the brand is known for. For affordable home furnishings with French flair, check out **Madura (40)** *(144 Newbury St., 617-267-0222, www.madurahome.com, M–Sa 10AM–7PM, Su noon–6PM)*. Thrift is a New England Yankee virtue, and even on Newbury Street, you can find a bargain. Just shop **Second Time Around (41)** *(176 Newbury St., 617-247-3504, www.secondtimearound.net, M–Sa 10AM–8PM, Su 11AM–7PM)*, an upscale consignment shop that carries like-new current-season designer clothing. Some of its merchandise also consists of end-of-season items from top retailers. You'll find Chanel, Gucci, Burberry, and other labels for a quarter to a third below original retail. There's a particularly good selection of evening dresses, designer jeans, handbags, and shoes as well. **Lester Harry's (42)** *(115 Newbury St., 617-927-5400, www.lesterharrys.com, M–Sa 10AM–6PM, Su noon–6PM)* is a one-stop shop for one-of-a-kind (albeit pricey) furnishings and clothing for babies to 'tweens. It's all things Jake at the flagship location of **Life is good (43)** *(285 Newbury St., 617-262-5068, www.lifeisgood.com, M–Sa 10AM–8PM, Su 11AM–6PM)*, carrying feel-good T-shirts, accessories, and more, featuring the smiling cartoon character and related designs. **344 (44)** *(344 Newbury St., 617-262-0400,* *www.shop344.com, M–Sa 10AM–8PM, Su 11AM–6PM)* a favorite among young fashionistas, is an exclusive, open-shelf boutique that offers up-to-the-minute super-cute casual clothes and accessories.

Trident Booksellers & Café (45) *(338 Newbury St., 617-267-8688, www.tridentbookscafe.com, daily 8AM–midnight)*, or simply "The Trident," is a fiercely independent bookstore that serves as a modern-day literary salon with lots of "meet the author events." Its wide-ranging magazine selection and its café, serving coffees, teas, wines, beers, and smoothies, plus a full menu and free Wi-Fi, encourages patrons to linger (and linger, and linger . . .). In business since 1796, **Shreve, Crump, & Low (46)** *(39 Newbury St., 617-267-9100, www.shrevecrumpandlow.com, M–W, F 10AM–6PM, Th 10AM–7PM, Sa 10AM–5PM, Su noon–5PM)* may be Boston's high society jeweler with a reputation for elegant jewelry, china, and silver. But it has a fantastic Boston giftware collection, including silver Swan Boat pins, a Red Sox money clip, and its signature "Gurgling Cod" ceramic pitcher. The glass-and-steel box of the **Apple (47)** *(815 Boylston St., 617-385-9400, www.apple.com, M–Sa 10AM–9PM, Su 11AM–7PM)* flagship store has made quite a splash in the staid Back Bay. Let your teens prowl **Newbury Comics (48)** *(332 Newbury St., 617-236-4930, www.newburycomics.com, M–Th 10AM–10PM, F–Sa 10AM–11PM, Su 10AM–8PM)* for CDs, comics, collectible action figures, and all things cool. Given that Boston weather can be bone-chilling cold in winter or sweltering in summer, an indoor mall can be a good thing. **Prudential Center (49)** *(800 Boylston St., 617-236-3100, www.prudentialcenter.*

com, M–Sa 10AM–9PM, Su 11AM–6PM) has over 70 stores, including Barnes & Noble, Ann Taylor, Free People, and Lacoste, as well as a food court. Posh **Copley Place (50)** *(100 Huntington Ave., 617-262-6600, www.shopcopley place.com, M–Sa 10AM–8PM, Su noon–6PM)*, another Back Bay shopping zone, is more up-market, with a Neiman Marcus, Tiffany & Co., Barneys, Jimmy Choo, and Louis Vuitton. A glass-covered pedestrian walkway connects the two malls.

WHERE TO STAY

Opposite the **Public Garden (1)**, the 1927 **Taj Boston (51)** **($$$-$$$$)** *(15 Arlington St., 617-536-5700, www.taj hotels.com)*, sets the standard for luxury with rooms furnished with antiques, luxurious fabrics, and marble-fitted baths. In the elegant setting of its French Room, a lavish afternoon tea is served on weekends at 2PM and 4PM. The **Four Seasons (52) ($$$$)** *(200 Boylston St., 617-338-4400, www.fourseasons.com/boston)* is known for its impeccable service and understated elegance. Business travelers and families appreciate the larger than average rooms, indoor pool, and fitness center at the **Hilton Back Bay (53) ($$$)** *(40 Dalton St., 617-236-1100, www.hilton.com)*. Overlooking the Boston Marathon finish line, the **Charlesmark Hotel (54) ($$)** *(655 Boylston St., 617-247-1212, www.charlesmarkhotel.com)* building dates from 1892 but the hotel offers a modern European sensibility. The value-priced **Newbury Guest House (55) ($$)** *(261 Newbury St., 617-670-6000, www.newburyguesthouse. com)* is a 32-room B&B set in three former Victorian residences. Enjoy fresh baked goods, yogurt, granola, or eggs and bacon in its sun-filled breakfast parlor. "Book 'em" takes on new meaning at **The Back Bay Hotel (56)** **($$$)** *(350 Stuart St., 617-266-7200, www.doylecollection. com)* formerly Jurys Boston, is situated in Boston's old police headquarters building. A property of Dublin-based hotel chain, The Doyle Collection, the ambience is modern yet comfortable, the hospitality genuine. Enjoy bites like beer-battered sausages along with pints and cocktails at its **Cuffs** bar. Wake up to an Irish breakfast at the **Stanhope Grill ($$)**. Rooms at the **Mandarin Oriental (57)** **($$$)** *(776 Boylston St., 617-535-8888, www.mandarin oriental.com/boston)* are among the most spacious in the city, with breathtaking bathrooms that include every amenity. At the 16,000-square-foot spa, the solicitous staff leaves you feeling as if you are their only guest. The Mandarin's signature restaurant, **Asana ($$)** offers both innovative New American cuisine and Asian-inspired dishes. **M Bar & Lounge** is one of the city's "in" spots and buzzes with assorted chic types. A Boston landmark hotel since 1912, the **Fairmont Copley Plaza (34) ($$$)** *(138 St. James Ave., 617-267-5300, www.fairmont.com/copley plaza)* has just undergone a $20 million renovation that preserves the romantic charm of its public spaces while giving the 338 rooms and suites a fresh update with new furnishings, flat screen TVs and a sophisticated plum and blue color scheme. The rooftop fitness center is impressive. Another exercise option? Take Catie, the hotel's resident black Labrador retriever, out for a walk around the city. At night, sip a dry martini in old-world style at the **Oak Bar** *(see page 129)*.

FENWAY/KENMORE SQUARE

Green Line "B," "C," or "D" to Kenmore Square Station, "D" to Fenway Station

• SNAPSHOT •

Created from marshy tidal flats in the late 1800s, the Frederick Law Olmsted-designed park known as the Back Bay Fens is the neighborhood's namesake. Of course, Fenway is probably most famous for its Temple of Baseball—Fenway Park. But the area is actually one of the city's most ethnically diverse residential neighborhoods and is the home (away from home) to a huge student population. Kenmore Square is the unofficial stomping ground for Boston University students.

It offers scores of restaurants, shops, and bars that cater to the college crowd. And then there's Lansdowne Street, lined with lively dance clubs and bars, another haunt of students as well as Red Sox fans.

PLACES TO SEE

Landmarks: The **Back Bay Fens (58)** *(bounded by Park Dr. and the Fenway, 617-635-4505, www.cityofboston.gov/parks/ emerald/, daily dawn–dusk)* is another link in Frederick Olmsted's Emerald Necklace *(see page 15)*. Created along the banks of the aptly-named Muddy River, the Back Bay Fens still retains a wild feel. Birders take note—the reedy marshes and flower and vegetable gardens make this a great spot for observing feathered friends. Stop and smell the roses at the **Kelleher Rose Garden (59)** *(mid-Fens, across from the Museum of Fine Arts)*. The **Fenway Victory Gardens (60)** *(main entrance at Boylston St. and Park Dr.)*, created during WWII, is America's oldest community garden. Sox fans mix with BU kids in the cafés and nightspots of busy **Kenmore Square (61)**. Since 1965, the square's red, white, and blue **CITGO Sign (62)** *(660 Beacon St., atop the Barnes & Noble Boston University Bookstore)* has been a beacon for weary Boston marathoners (it marks the 25th mile), Lansdowne Street nightclubbers, and Red Sox fans (every time a home run soars over Fenway Park's left field Green Monster, it's seen by countless fans watching the game on TV; hence the sign's nickname "see-it-go."). Once dubbed an "object d'heart" by *Time* magazine, the double-faced sign measures 60 feet by 60 feet.

Arts & Entertainment:

Baseball fans of all persuasions wax rhapsodic about ★**FENWAY PARK (63)** *(4 Yawkey Way, 617-226-6666, www.fenwaypark.com, M–F 10AM–5PM, same hours weekends when there is a game)*, beloved home of the Boston Red Sox. This is the major league's oldest ballpark—its first game took place on April 9, 1912 (Red Sox vs. Harvard), and its first professional game was April 20, 1912 (Red Sox vs. New York Highlanders, now the New York Yankees; Sox won, 7–6 in 11 innings). Guided tours

TOP PICK!

are offered daily, year-round. Hear Red Sox lore about Cy Young, Babe Ruth, Ted Williams, and more; touch the Green Monster (Fenway's infamous left field wall); and take in the view from the press box. Tours leave from the **Souvenir Store** *(19 Yawkey Way, 617-226-6666, http:// boston.redsox.mlb.com/bos/ballpark/tour.jsp, summer daily 9AM–4PM, check Web site for winter hours)*. Note: The last tour on a game day starts three hours before the game and is shorter than regular tours. Scoring tickets to a Red Sox game is tough, although a limited number of game-day tickets (including standing room and scattered single seats) go on sale at Gate E on Lansdowne Street two hours before game time. You may line up no earlier than five hours prior to game time, and you must enter the ballpark immediately after purchase. If you're lucky enough to see a game, make sure your experience includes a real "Fenway Frank" hot dog, paired with a Samuel Adams.

PLACES TO EAT AND DRINK
Where to Eat:

Recover from baseball-induced high spirits at New American bistro **Eastern Standard (64) ($$)** *(528 Commonwealth Ave., 617-532-9100, www.easternstandard boston.com, Su–Th 7AM–1:30AM, F–Sa 7AM–1:30AM)*. Menu offerings include oysters, burgers, and other stand-bys, as well as (for the gastronomically intrepid) "Today's Offal." In balmy weather, dine al fresco on the patio. With juicy burgers ground fresh daily, fries and onion rings hand-cut, and frappes made to order, **UBurger (65) ($)** *(636 Beacon St., 617-536-0448, www.uburgerboston.com, M–Sa 11AM–11PM, Su noon–11PM)* is a classic. Try the "Boom Burger" with fried jalapeños, cheddar cheese, lettuce, tomato, and chipotle sauce. Kenmore Square goes uptown with **Petit Robert Bistro (66) ($$)** *(468 Commonwealth Ave., 617-375-0699, www.petitrobertbistro.com, daily 11AM–11PM)*, a cozy, two-story town house charmer. The menu features French dishes in all their hearty simplicity. **Uni (67) ($$)** *(307A Commonwealth Ave. 617-536-7200, www.uni sashimibar.com, Su–Th 5:30PM–10PM, F–Sa 5:30PM–10:30PM)* is a small gem of a bar that offers pristine and inventive sashimi. **Trattoria Toscana (68) ($$)** *(130 Jersey St., 617-247-9508, M–Sa 5PM–10PM)* is a sweet little spot for authentic Italian. Be sure to have the house antipasti and someone at your table must order the gnocchi.

Bars & Nightlife:

The **House of Blues (69)** *(15 Lansdowne St., 888-693-2583, www.houseofblues.com; box office opens 1 hour before showtime)* has returned to Boston—the original HOB opened in Cambridge in 1992, but closed several years ago. Relocated next to Fenway Park in 2009, this two-level club is the largest concert venue in the city. **The Hawthorne (70)** *(Hotel Commonwealth, 500 Commonwealth Ave., 617-532-9150, www.thehawthorne bar.com, daily 5PM–2AM)* draws a 30-something-and-up nocturnal crowd with craft cocktails and upscale bar food like tuna on wheat with shallot jam. Farther along Commonwealth, you'll find Boston's **Paradise** *(967-969 Commonwealth Ave., 617-562-8800, www.thedise.com; box office M–Sa noon–6PM)* club, where U2 played its first U.S. concert performance. The club still stages hot national and up-and-coming acts, while its more sub-dued next-door lounge features indie singer/songwriters.

Sleek **Audubon Circle (71)** *(838 Beacon St., 617-421-1910, www.auduboncircle.us, M–Sa 11:30AM–1AM, Su 11AM–1AM)* attracts unpretentious patrons with its able service, beer selection, specialty cocktails, and one of Boston's best burgers. **Game On! (72)** *(82 Lansdowne St., 617-351-7001, www.gameonboston.com, Su–M 11:30AM–1AM, Tu–Sa 11:30AM–2AM)* is sports fan central. This two-story, multimedia bar offers nearly 100 high-def screens, decent food, and a dance floor. Can't snag tickets to the game? Built into the side of Fenway Park with a giant window that overlooks center field, a trip to the **Bleacher Bar (72)** *(82 Lansdowne St., 617-262-2424, www.bleacherbarboston.com, Su–W 11AM–1AM, Th–Sa 11AM–2AM)* may be the next best thing.

WHERE TO STAY

Independent luxury **Hotel Commonwealth (73) ($$$)** *(500 Commonwealth Ave., 617-933-5000, www.hotel commonwealth.com)* offers beautifully appointed rooms (some overlook either Fenway Park or Commonwealth Avenue) in a new-ish building at Kenmore Square. Here you'll find three of Boston's most talked-about dining spots: **Island Creek Oyster Bar**, **Eastern Standard (64)**, and **The Hawthorne (70)**. Recently named the No. 1 small city hotel in the U.S. and Canada by *Travel + Leisure* readers, **The Eliot Hotel (74) ($$$)** *(370 Commonwealth Ave., 617-267-1607, www.eliothotel.com)* is exquisite with one-of-a-kind rooms and a residential feel. For dining choose between **Clio**, Ken Oringer's temple to haute French cuisine, and the much acclaimed sashimi bar **Uni (67)**.

chapter 7

SOUTH END

HUNTINGTON AVENUE/
AVENUE OF THE ARTS

SOUTH END

HUNTINGTON AVENUE/ AVENUE OF THE ARTS

Places to See:

1. Cathedral of the Holy Cross
2. Cyclorama
3. Boston Ballet
4. Union Park
5. Peters Park
6. Carroll and Sons
7. Bromfield Gallery
8. Boston Sculptors Gallery
9. Wally's Café
32. Christian Science Plaza
33. MUSEUM OF FINE ARTS ★
34. ISABELLA STEWART GARDNER MUSEUM ★
35. Massachusetts College of Art
36. Symphony Hall
37. Jordan Hall
38. Boston University Theatre

Places to Eat & Drink:

10. b. good
11. Charlie's Sandwich Shoppe
12. Red Lantern
13. South End Buttery
14. Orinoco
15. Picco
16. Flour Bakery + Café
17. Tremont 647
18. Oishii
19. Aquitaine
20. Twentyeight Degrees
21. Delux Café & Lounge
22. Club Café
23. Salty Pig
39. Brasserie JO
40. Betty's Wok & Noodle Diner
41. Moby Dick
42. Buloco
43. Garden Cafeteria
44. Bravo
45. RTP

★ *Top Pick*

Where to Shop:

Where to Stay:

"Clear out 800,000 people and preserve it as a museum piece."

—Frank Lloyd Wright on the city of Boston

Orange Line to Back Bay Station

• SNAPSHOT •

Not to be confused with South Boston, or "Southie," the South End is just a short walk from Back Bay and downtown. Like the Back Bay, the South End was built on swampland and landfill in the late 1800s. Scores of brick townhomes, many with cast-iron scroll railings and decorative balconies, were constructed and many

remain; in fact, you'll find the largest intact Victorian row-house neighborhood in the U.S. here. The South End is home to a large gay population, a vibrant Hispanic community, and a historical African American presence. Thanks to residents' revitalization efforts, it's become one of Boston's

most desirable neighborhoods. Professionals and empty nesters are attracted to its London-style park squares, tree-lined streets, and retail and restaurant scene. Gallery lovers also find a lot to like about the area south of Washington—"SoWa" to those in the know.

PLACES TO SEE
Landmarks:

Dedicated in 1875, the **Cathedral of the Holy Cross (1)** *(1400 Washington St., 617-542-5682, www.holycross boston.com)* is the seat of the Archdiocese of Boston.

The cathedral is the largest church in New England; it's larger than St. Patrick's in New York City. Constructed of local Roxbury puddingstone, it's resplendent with its historic stained-glass windows and mighty Hook & Hastings organ. The circular-shaped, copper-topped **Cyclorama (2)** *(539 Tremont St., 617-426-5000, www.bcaonline.org, M–F 9AM–5PM)* is the centerpiece of the four-acre **Boston Center for the Arts** complex. It was built in the late 1800s to house a 360-degree mural of the Battle of Gettysburg. (Such panoramic paintings, also called cycloramas, were popular in the 19th century.) Today the structure is a venue for craft and antique shows, weddings, and corporate events. The BCA is home to numerous theater companies and arts organizations; its dynamic campus includes performance spaces, galleries, and studios showcasing performing and visual art. The five-story, Graham Gund-designed building at the corner of Warren and Clarendon, for example, is the headquarters of the **Boston Ballet (3)** *(19 Clarendon St., 617-695-6950, www.bostonballet.org)*, among the top ballet companies in the world.

Charming **Union Park (4)** *(bordered by Waltham, Shawmut Ave., Dedham, and Tremont Sts.)* with its bow-fronted townhomes, gated oval of grass, and flower-surrounded fountain, is reminiscent of green spaces of London. Dog-friendly South End is home to the city's first officially

sanctioned canine run: Joe Wex Dog Recreation Space at **Peters Park (5)** *(bet. Washington St. and Shawmut Ave., www.peterspark.org).*

Arts & Entertainment:

Carroll and Sons (6) *(450 Harrison Ave., 617-482-2477, www.carrollandsons.net, Tu–Sa 10AM–6PM)* is one of Boston's big-name mainstream galleries, showcasing a nice mix of new and established contemporary artists. In the same building, **Bromfield Gallery (7)** *(450 Harrison Ave., 617-451-3605, www.bromfieldgallery.com, W–Sa noon–5PM)*, the city's oldest artist-owned co-op, has two gallery spaces presenting visual art in all forms of media. Exhibits change on a monthly basis. The acclaimed **Boston Sculptors Gallery (8)** *(486 Harrison Ave., 617-482-7781, www.bostonsculptors.com, W–Su noon–6PM)* is an artists' cooperative exclusively for sculptors. It hosts two shows each month, presenting members' works, plus a holiday group show in December. An appreciative crowd gathers for live music 365 days a year at historic jazz haunt **Wally's Café (9)** *(427 Massachusetts Ave., 617-424-1408, www.wallyscafe.com, M–Sa 11AM–2AM, Su noon–2AM, Sa–Su jam 5PM–8PM)*, founded in 1947 by Joseph L. Walcott. The café showcases and nurtures aspiring local musicians, many from the Berklee School of Music *(see page 125).*

PLACES TO EAT & DRINK
Where to Eat:

The South End is a destination dining spot. Tremont Street is known as "Restaurant Row," but there are lots of inexpensive neighborhood eateries, too. Boston buzzes about **The Beehive ($$)** *(541 Tremont St., 617-423-0069, www.beehiveboston.com, M–F 3PM–2AM, Sa–Su 10:30AM–2AM)*, located in the "underbelly" of the **Cyclorama (2)**. It offers a sultry setting, live music, chic cocktails, and swell food. The global menu changes regularly and there are always interesting platters to share. Popular **b. good (10) ($)** *(131 Dartmouth St., 617-424-5252, www.bgood.com, M–Sa 11AM–10PM, Su 11AM–9PM)* is a hip fast-food eatery that emphasizes lower-fat shakes and smoothies, grease-free burgers, and sandwiches, all made on the premises with fresh ingredients. Calorie and nutrition information is printed on the menu. Free wireless available. **Charlie's Sandwich Shoppe (11) ($)** *(429 Columbus Ave., 617-536-7669, M–F 6AM–2:30PM, Sa 7:30AM–1PM, closed Su)*

has been a South End institution since 1927. Open for breakfast and lunch only, this old-fashioned diner is famous for its oversized omelets and turkey hash with eggs. Be prepared for a wait, bring cash, and please note: no patron bathrooms. Enjoy modern Pan-Asian tastes like lobster rangoon, duck buns, and Singapore street noodles at **Red Lantern (12) ($$)** *(39 Stanhope St., 617-262-3900, redlanternboston.com, daily 5PM–1AM)* in a Vegas-like setting decorated with giant Buddhas and oversized lanterns. At night a see-and-be-seen crowd packs the 40-foot bar. Bright, cheery **South End Buttery (13) ($)** *(314 Shawmut Ave., 617-482-1015,* *www.southendbuttery.com; café daily 6:30AM–8PM, bistro Su–W 5:30PM–10PM, Th–Sa 5:30PM–11PM)* is just the spot for morning muffins and cappuccinos. Recently expanded, the Buttery now has a dining room with table service and offers bistro fare at prices modest for the neighborhood. Combining the flavors of the Andes and the Caribbean, **Orinoco (14) ($$)** *(477 Shawmut Ave., 617-369-7075, www.orinocokitchen.com, Tu–W noon–2:30PM, 6PM–10PM, Th–Sa noon–2:30PM, 6PM–11PM, Su 11AM–3PM)* offers zesty cuisine inspired by Venezuela's *taguaritas*—rustic roadside eateries. Its beef-, pork-, chicken-, and cheese-filled corn pocketlike *arepas* are a must-try. Complement your meal with a tropical fruit drink or glass of South American wine. **Picco (15) ($)** *(513 Tremont St., 617-927-0066, www.piccorestaurant.com, Su–W 11AM–10PM, Th–Sa 11AM–11PM)*, "Pizza & Ice Cream Company," is the place for South End-style arugula/goat cheese pizza and honey ice cream. Everything is made right here with quality ingredients. The wine and beer list has been specially selected to pair with its menu. Stop by **Flour Bakery + Café (16) ($)** *(1595 Washington St., 617-267-4300, www.flourbakery.com, M–F 7AM–9PM, Sa 8AM–6PM, Su 8AM–4PM)* for sinful home-style baked goods—owner Joanne Chang's sticky buns recently triumphed in a "throw-down" against celebrity chef Bobby Flay. The made-to-order sandwiches are exceptional, too. Trendy **Tremont 647 (17) ($$)** *(647 Tremont St., 617-266-4600, www.tremont647.com, M–Th 5:30PM–10PM, F 5:30PM–11PM, Sa 10:30AM–2PM, 5:30PM–10PM, Su 10:30AM–3PM, 5:30PM–10PM)* features "adventurous American cuisine." Chef/owner Andy Husband's signature appetizer, "Too Stinky Cheeses," with truffle honey and house-made jams on grilled toast, pretty much qualifies in that regard. Entrées include wood-grilled BBQ Alaskan salmon with Swiss chard and potato salad with a warm bacon vinaigrette. Dessert? Try "Almost Famous Donuts," with mascarpone-Nutella cream. Their weekend brunch is a South End event—and the staff wears their pajamas. Get your fish fix at **Oishii (18) ($$$)** *(1166 Washington St., 617-482-8868, www.oishiiboston.com, Tu-Sa noon–3PM, 5:30PM–midnight, Su 1PM–10PM)*, excelling at familiar and creative sushi, sashimi, and maki creations. On the short list for best French bistro fare in the South End: acclaimed **Aquitaine (19) ($$$)** *(569 Tremont St., 617-424-8577, www.aquitaineboston.com, M-W 11:30AM–3PM, 5:30PM–10PM, Th-F 11:30AM–3PM, 5:30PM–11PM, Sa 10AM–3PM, 5:30PM–11PM, Su 10AM–3PM, 5:30PM–10PM)*. Decor includes warm, earthy hues, white linen-topped tables, and leather booths. The menu features Gallic classics with a twist, like roasted natural chicken, fingerlings, asparagus and haricots verts ragoût, and lemon thyme pan drippings. Tip: On a budget? Try lunch here; the daily special includes soup, a salad, a sandwich, and a drink at a very good price.

Bars & Nightlife:

Twentyeight Degrees (20) *(1 Appleton St., 617-728-0728, www.28degrees-boston.com, Su-W 5PM–midnight, Th-Sa 5PM–1AM)* is a chic lounge with a nice selection of cocktails. Dreamy Bellinis are a specialty, as is the elderflower daiquiri and a delicious Plum and Ginger cocktail with fresh lime. Jazzy, soulful, and down tempo grooves spin at a conversational level. Funky **Delux Café & Lounge (21)** *(100 Chandler St., 617-338-5258, M–Sa 5PM–1AM)*, with its Elvis shrine and permanent Christmas decorations, is an old-school dive that attracts a mix of patrons: working class folk, yuppies, and beatniks.

Drink prices are reasonable and the grilled cheese sandwiches famous. Cash only. **Club Café (22)** *(209 Columbus Ave., 617-536-0966, www.clubcafe.com, M–W 4PM–1AM, Th–Su noon–2AM)* is one of the city's leading gay and lesbian clubs. It has a large dance floor, and its restaurant serves American bistro cuisine for dinner and Sunday brunch comfort classics on weekend mornings. Near the Back Bay T station, the **Salty Pig (23)** *(130 Dartmouth St., 617-536-6200, www.thesaltypig.com, daily 11AM–1AM)* is a spirited spot that fills with locals and visitors chatting over craft beer and wine while sampling from made-to-order charcuterie boards and slices of thin-crust pizzas.

WHERE TO SHOP

Like brunch, the **South End Open Market (24)** *(540 Harrison Ave., 617-481-2257, www.southendopenmarket. com, mid-May–mid-Oct, Su 10AM–4PM)*, aka "SoWa Open Market," is a Sunday tradition. Look for the rows of white tents, under which you'll discover antiques, collectibles, crafts, clothing, jewelry, artwork, baked goods, preserves,

149

garden plants, and much more. Here, too, some of New England's hippest farmers purvey fresh veggies, fruits, and cheeses. Of late, Boston has experienced an explosion in gourmet food trucks, and SoWa is home to a rotating line-up of the city's best. Standouts include Roxy's Gourmet Grilled Cheese, Lincoln Street Coffee, and the Cupcakory. **Lekker Unique Home Furnishings (25)** *(1317 Washington St., www.lekkerhome.com, M 10AM–6PM, Tu–F 10AM–7PM, Sa 11AM–6PM, Su noon–5PM)* gets its name from a Dutch word meaning "alluring, enticing, and tempting," which well defines this store's collection of stylish gifts and contemporary lifestyle accessories. Owner Jill Goldberg's dog is often in residence at **Hudson (26)** *(312 Shawmut Ave., 617-292-0900, www.hudson-boston.com, M–W, F, Sa 10AM–6PM, Th 10AM–7PM, Su 11AM–5PM)*, where you'll find modern and vintage home furnishings imaginatively displayed. Fashion-forward men will appreciate the utilitarian, urban-casual apparel

and accessories at **Uniform (27)** *(511 Tremont St., 617-247-2360, www.uniformboston.com, Tu–W 11AM–7PM, Th–Sa 11AM–8PM, Su noon–5PM)*; the store also carries skin care products for both sexes. **Sooki (28)** *(505 Tremont St., 617-536-0809, www.sookiboston.com, Tu–Sa 11AM–6PM, Su noon–5PM)* stocks handpicked, one-of-a-kind women's clothing pieces, shoes, accessories, and jewelry by designers and artists from around the planet. Find timeless and chic women's wear at **Sara Campbell (29)** *(44 Plympton St., 617-482-7272,* *www.saracampbell.com, M–F 10AM–5:30PM, Sa 10AM–5PM).* Looks range from everyday casual to special occasion, often in bright colors and with unexpected and intricate detail.

WHERE TO STAY

Boutique hotel **Chandler Inn (30) ($$)** *(26 Chandler St., 617-482-3450, www.chandlerinn.com)* is convenient and charming. In recent years all of the hotel's 50 guest rooms have undergone a facelift, and now boast high design elements including mod furnishings and marble baths with walk-in showers. **Fritz Lounge ($-$$)** *(617-482-4428, www.fritzboston.com, daily noon–2AM),* the gay sports bar on the first floor, is another draw, especially for its weekend brunches. A favorite hotel for budget-minded hipsters, The **Inn @ St. Botolph (31) ($$)** *(99 St. Botolph, 617-236-8099, www.innatstbotolph. com)* is a boutique hotel located in a brownstone beauty. Each suite is equipped with a kitchenette plus 42-inch HD TVs, and there is a gym on-site. Enjoy a complimentary continental breakfast in the lounge in front of a fireplace.

HUNTINGTON AVENUE/
AVENUE OF THE ARTS

*Green Line "E" Train to Symphony, Northeastern
University, or Museum of Fine Arts Stations*

• SNAPSHOT •

Huntington Avenue is the major thoroughfare spanning
the Back Bay and Fenway neighborhoods. The middle
section of Huntington—from Massachusetts Avenue to
Brigham Circle—is also known as the "Avenue of the
Arts" and is home to several renowned cultural organizations, including the Museum of Fine Arts and
Symphony Hall. The New England Conservatory,
Northeastern University, and Wentworth
Institute of Technology front this section
of Huntington Avenue as well. Many of
the pubs and pizza places dotting the
area cater to the local college crowd.
Interesting ethnic eateries have lately
opened here, too. In recent years, the
city has spruced up the avenue by plant-
ing trees and installing landscaping and new
lighting, much appreciated by the tourists, students, and
culture aficionados frequenting the area day and night.

PLACES TO SEE
Landmarks:

The **Christian Science Plaza (32)** *(175 Huntington Ave., 617-450-2000, www.tfccs.com)*, designed in the 1960s by the I. M. Pei firm (of Louvre pyramid and JFK Library fame), is world headquarters for the First Church of Christ, Scientist, founded by Mary Baker Eddy in 1879. Its 686-foot reflecting pool and colon-nade are illuminated at night, mak-ing this an ideal spot for an evening stroll. In summer, children cavort in the 80-foot-diameter water fountain at the plaza's end. On site is the Romanesque **Mother Church**, which contains one of the largest pipe organs in the world (13,290 pipes),  and 1901 **Horticultural Hall** *(Massachusetts and Huntington Aves.)*, former home of the Massachusetts Horticultural Society and a Beaux Arts beauty (notice the garland swags over the windows).

Arts & Entertainment:

Boston's must-see **★MUSEUM OF FINE ARTS (33)** *(465 Huntington Ave., 617-267-9300, www.mfa.org, M–Tu 10AM–4:45PM, W–F 10AM–9:45PM, Sa–Su 10AM–4:45PM)* is a

TOP PICK!

treasure trove of 400,000 objects. Its holdings include what is considered the best assemblage of Japanese art outside the Land of the Rising Sun and European mas-terpieces from the 7th through the late 20th centuries, including the most Monets outside Paris. In late 2010, the MFA unveiled its Art of the Americas Wing, a stunning four-story gallery space that brings together the museum's extensive holdings of North, South, and Central American art. The American collection includes paintings by Edward Hopper, Winslow Homer, John Singleton Copley, and John Singer Sargent (the MFA's Huntington Street entrance rotunda also features specially-commissioned paintings by Sargent), folk art, colonial portraits, decorative arts, furniture, and silver items smithed by Paul Revere, including his iconic *Sons of Liberty Bowl*. You'll also find objects from the ancient world: Egypt's Old Kingdom, Nubia, the Near East, Cyprus, Greece, Etruria, and Rome; works from Oceania and Africa; prints, drawings, and photographs (Durer, Rembrandt, Picasso, Munch, and Stieglitz); textiles and costumes; and a notable collection of antique musical instruments. Tip: General admission includes a second visit within a 10-day period. In 2011, the MFA completed the renovation of its West Wing, consolidating its contemporary art collection, which spans the 1950s to the present.

Not exactly on Huntington Avenue but certainly "of" the Avenue of the Arts is the ★**ISABELLA STEWART GARDNER MUSEUM (34)** *(280 The Fenway, 617-566-1401, www.gardnermuseum.org, W, F–M 11AM–5PM, Th 11AM–9PM, closed Tu)*.

TOP PICK!

Socialite Isabella Stewart Gardner constructed her 1903 Boston residence in the style of a 15th-century Venetian palazzo, with an enclosed courtyard, and filled it with masterpieces. Upon her passing in 1924, her will decreed that everything remain as she left it "for the education and enrichment of the public" (and that admission be forever free to anyone named "Isabella"). It makes for an exquisite setting in which to experience Gardner's personal collection of European, Asian, and American paintings, sculpture, textiles, ceramics, furniture, illuminated manuscripts, and other artifacts. Highlights include Titian's *Europa*, Botticelli's *Tragedy of Lucretia*, Rembrandt's *Self-Portrait, Age 23*, plus works by Raphael, Matisse, and Mrs. Gardner's own friends, Whistler and John Singer Sargent. With the opening of a dazzling steel, glass, and copper Renzo Piano–designed wing in 2012, the footprint of the Gardner has more than doubled. The addition includes an expanded entrance, gallery space for temporary exhibitions, and the state-of-the-art Calderwood Performance Hall *(617-278-5150)*. Flowers bloom year-round in the **courtyard** (quite a feat considering Boston's winter weather), and in April, nasturtiums are hung from the balconies to honor Mrs. Gardner's April 14th birthday. Lunch and desserts are served at the **Café G ($)**. Tip: Visitors who've been to the **Museum of Fine Arts (33)** *(see page 153)* within the past two days receive a $2 admission discount.

Galleries at the **Massachusetts College of Art (35)** *(621 Huntington Ave., 617-879-7000, www.massart.edu/ galleries; there are several galleries throughout the campus, hours vary)* offer free exhibitions of students' work and that of more established artists; they're definitely worth a walk-through. Historic **Symphony Hall (36)** *(301 Massachusetts Ave., 617-266-1492, www.bso.org, box office open M–F 10AM–6PM, Sa noon–6PM, and through intermission on concert evenings)* opened with an inaugural concert by the Boston Symphony Orchestra on October 15, 1900. Today **Symphony Hall** is home to both the **Boston Symphony Orchestra** and the **Boston Pops**. For classical music lovers, attending a BSO performance here is a sublime experience—the acoustics are incomparable. Tours of hall public spaces and selected behind-the-scenes areas are offered from October to June; call for details. For those with more eclectic tastes, the Boston Pops presents a holiday music program in December and jazz, light classical, and even rock programs in May and June.

One of the most acoustically perfect spaces in the world, 100-year-old **Jordan Hall (37)** *(30 Gainsborough St., 617-585-1260, www.necmusic.edu; box office M–F 10AM–6PM, Sa noon–6PM, and 1-1/2 hrs. before performances)*, the New England Conservatory's principal performance space, hosts almost daily—and mostly free—student and faculty performances of classical, jazz, and contemporary music. Before premiering in the Big Apple, hit plays make it big first at the **Boston University Theatre (38)** *(264 Huntington Ave., 617-266-0800, www.huntingtontheatre. org; box office Tu–Th noon–7:30PM, F–Sa noon–8PM, Su noon–4PM)*, principal home of the **Huntington Theatre Company** which presents new plays and new productions of stage classics in an intimate setting.

Kids:

Walk across a 30-foot glass bridge to the middle of the world at the **Mapparium** in the **Mary Baker Eddy Library** *(200 Massachusetts Ave., 617-450-7000, www.marybakereddy library.org, Tu–Su 10AM–4PM)* at **Christian Science Plaza (32)** *(see page 153)*. A three-story, stained-glass globe, it offers a snapshot of the world in 1935, when the globe was constructed. In the library's **Hall of Ideas**, an intriguing glass-and-bronze fountain by sculptor Howard Ben Tré bubbles with quotations by influential minds. Computer programming by MIT grad and media designer David Small enables the words to move around the rim and "overflow" onto floor and walls. Art museums can be intimidating to kids, but the **Museum of Fine Arts (33)** has programs that make art fun and accessible. Self-guided activity booklets are available at the information center. Check for children's art workshops, too.

PLACES TO EAT & DRINK
Where to Eat:

With its sophisticated setting and French bistro fare, acclaimed **Brasserie JO (39) ($$)** *(Colonnade Hotel, 120 Huntington Ave., 617-425-3240, www.brasseriejoboston.com, M–T 10AM–1AM, W–Su 8AM–midnight)* offers a no-fail dining experience. Try the onion tarte, Parisian steak, or the house "Hopla" Alsatian-style draft beer. Its chocolate mousse is divine. Brassiere Jo is open for breakfast and weekend brunch, too. Popular "Chinese retro" **Betty's Wok & Noodle Diner (40) ($-$$)** *(250 Huntington Ave., 617-424-1950, www.bettyswokandnoodle.com, Su–M 11:30AM–9PM, Tu–Th 11:30AM–10PM, F–Sa 11:30AM–11PM)* is all about Asian/Latino fusion—think pressed sandwiches with Cuban coleslaw and special sauce, or Won-Ton Pollo Taco, wok-tossed chicken with red peppers, onions, and garlic served with brown rice, black beans, cheddar cheese, and hot-and-sour sauce. Signature sake cocktails include the Tokyo Manhattan, Bettypolitan, and the Saketini. **Moby Dick (41) ($)** *(269 Huntington Ave., 617-236-5511, Tu–Sa 11AM–10:30PM, Su noon–9:30PM)* is located on the same block as **Symphony Hall (36)** *(see page 155)*; you may very well eat your saffron chicken kebab next to an orchestra member. Cash only. For quick, tasty, healthful wraps, burritos, soups, salads, and smoothies, try acclaimed, locally-owned chain **Boloco (42) ($)** *(359-369 Huntington Ave., Marino Ctr., 617-536-6814, M–F 8AM–10PM, Sa–Su 9AM–9PM)*. Got a case of museum munchies? Head downstairs to the family-friendly **Garden Cafeteria (43) ($)** *(Museum of Fine Arts, West Wing, court level, 465 Huntington Ave., 617-369-3474, www.mfa.org, daily 10:30AM–4PM)* at the **Museum of Fine Arts (33)** for sandwiches, pizza, salads, or coffee. If the weather is good, take it outside. For inspired dining, the MFA's **Bravo (44) ($$)** *(Museum of Fine Arts, Upper Level Galleria, West Wing, 465 Huntington Ave., 617-369-3474, www.mfa.org, M–Tu 11:30AM–3PM, W–F 11:30AM–3PM, 5:30PM–8:30PM, Sa–Su 11:30AM–3PM)* offers cocktails, wine tastings, and eclectic cuisine in surrounds that feature rotating masterpieces from the museum's modern and contemporary collections. Superbly situated in the courtyard of the Art of the Americas Wing, the **New American Café ($$)** offers simple but exemplary regional American fare: salads, soups, sandwiches and entrées (try the seafood pot pie), desserts, and coffee.

Bars & Nightlife:

Boston's buffest bods spend the summer at the **RTP (45)** ("Roof Top Pool," *Colonnade Hotel, 120 Huntington Ave., 617-424-7000, www.colonnadehotel.com/roof_top_pool, Memorial Day–Labor Day, open to the public M–F 8AM–8PM, weather permitting)*, named a Best Poolside Bar by *Playboy* Online A-List for its cocktails, clubhouse setting, exclusive concerts, and killer views.

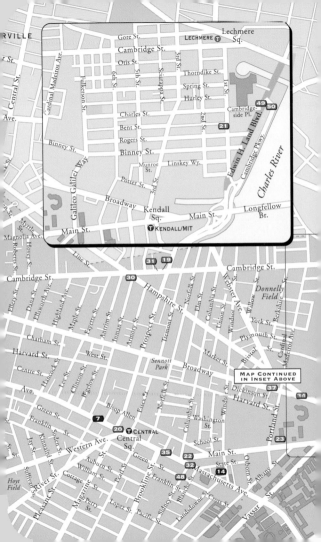

WHERE TO SHOP

The **Bookstore** and **Gift Shop** at the **Museum of Fine Arts (33)** *(617-369-3575, www.mfashop.com)* boasts the largest selection of art books in New England and quality gift items you won't find anywhere else, from magnets, mugs, and tote bags, to sculpture, music boxes, dinnerware, jewelry, apparel, and educational games and toys for kids. There is a tasteful selection of Boston-themed gifts, too. At the **Gift Shop** of the **Isabella Stewart Gardner Museum (34)** *(617-278-5180, www.gift.gardnermuseum.org)* you'll also find a nice array of arts-related books, gifts, posters, prints, and more. The storefront for **Bodega (46)** *(6 Clearway St., 617-421-1550, www.bdgastore.com, M–Th 11AM–6PM, F–Sa 11AM–7PM)* is just that—a front. Behind the vending machine is a high-end boutique that sells trendy sneakers—limited edition Nike, Puma, and Warrior footwear.

WHERE TO STAY

Frank Sinatra, Dean Martin, Shirley MacLaine, Matt Damon, Ronald Reagan, and other notables have stayed at Colonnade Hotel (47) ($$$) *(120 Huntington Ave., 617-424-7000, www.colonnadehotel.com)*, known for its personal service and luxurious accommodations. Rooms evoke contemporary European style and come with plush robes and rubber duckies. Accommodations have recently been updated at the MidTown Hotel (48) ($) *(220 Huntington Ave., 617-262-1000, www.midtownhotel.com)*, a budget-friendly choice. There's an outdoor pool in season, on-site beauty salon, and value-priced parking.

chapter 8

CAMBRIDGE HIGHLIGHTS

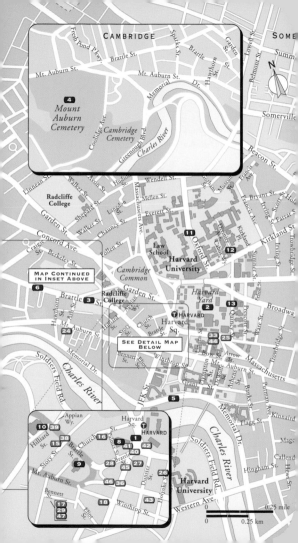

CAMBRIDGE HIGHLIGHTS

Places to See:

1. Harvard Square
2. Harvard Yard
3. "Tory Row"
4. Mount Auburn Cemetery
5. Memorial Drive
6. Longfellow House-
   Washington Headquarters
   National Historic Site
7. Cantab Lounge
8. Club Passim
9. Brattle Theatre
10. American Repertory Theatre
11. Harvard Museum of
    Natural History
12. Peabody Museum of
    Archaeology & Ethnology
13. Harvard Art Museum
14. MIT Museum

Places to Eat & Drink:

15. Café Algiers
16. Border Café
17. Henrietta's Table
18. Upstairs on the Square
19. East Coast Grill
    and Raw Bar
20. India Pavilion
21. Helmand
22. Toscanini's
23. Area Four

24. Darwin's Ltd.
25. Mr. Bartley's Burger
26. Sandrines
27. Sweet
28. Bertucci's
29. Regattabar
30. Ryles Jazz Club
31. Bukowski's Tavern
32. Middlesex Lounge
33. Hong Kong
34. Flat-Top Johnny's
35. Middle East

Where to Shop:

36. Hootenanny at the Garage
37. Garment District
38. Colonial Drug
39. L. A. Burdick
40. Black Ink
41. Harvard Coop
42. Out of Town News
43. Schoenhof's
44. Grolier Poetry Book Shop
45. Curious George
46. The Million Year Picnic

Where to Stay:

47. The Charles Hotel
48. Le Meridien Cambridge-MIT
49. Hotel Marlowe
50. Royal Sonesta Hotel

Red Line to Harvard Square Station

• SNAPSHOT •

Originally called "Newtowne," ★**CAMBRIDGE**, just across the Charles River from Boston, was later renamed after the British university town. The New World version is of course also a university town, being home to both Harvard and MIT. With cafés, colorful bars, and quirky shops and bookstores, this lively enclave, often called Boston's "Left Bank," attracts not only scholars, but also activists, bohemians, and a diverse, multicultural population.

Strike up a conversation with a local or two and you'll find that "Cantabrigians" revel in their roles as left-leaning thinkers and are eager to expound their views.

PLACES TO SEE
Landmarks:

It's hip to be square. **Harvard Square (1)** *(Massachusetts Ave., Brattle St., and John F. Kennedy St., 617-491-3434, www.harvardsquare.com)* is the place for people-watching. College students (both slackers and keeners), professors, beatniks, runaways, missionaries, and protesters are all part of the passing parade, along with evening/weekend street performers and resident chess masters awaiting challengers at the square's permanent chess tables. The adjacent **Harvard Yard (2)** *(bordered by Massachusetts Ave. and Peabody, Cambridge, Quincy, and Harvard Sts.)* is the traditional center of university life and the oldest part of campus. Enter at **Johnston Gate** *(Massachusetts Ave.)*; there's something about the ivy-covered red brick buildings, manicured lawns, and leafy trees that makes you feel smarter just walking through here. Daniel Chester French's 1884 **statue of John Harvard**, inscribed "John Harvard, Founder, 1638," is also known as the "Statue of Three Lies." Why? Consider . . . there are no known portraits of Harvard (the statue actually depicts a student model), Harvard was not a founder, and the university was actually founded in 1636. You might think twice before rubbing the statue's left foot for luck as visitors are typically encouraged to do; rumor has it undergrads urinate here, too. Stroll the elegant mansions of **"Tory Row" (3)** *(Brattle St.)*; they date from the 1700s. The street's nickname comes from its original Loyalist residents. Inspired by Paris's Père Lachaise, **Mount Auburn Cemetery (4)** *(580 Mt. Auburn St., 617-547-7105, www.mountauburn.org, daily 8AM–5PM, summer 8AM–7PM)* is a scenic delight—meticulously landscaped grounds, fountains, and pathways, all in grand Victorian tradition. This is the final resting place for many history makers, including Winslow Homer, Henry Wadsworth Longfellow, Mary Baker Eddy, Isabella Stewart Gardner, Fannie Farmer, and Charles Bulfinch. Enjoy views of Boston and Cambridge from the cemetery's tower (entrance is free during the summer). Walkers (no jogging or cycling allowed) regularly enjoy its tranquil paths. Maps are available at the main gatehouse. To the delight of walkers, runners, and cyclists, the city closes **Memorial Drive (5)** *(bet. Western Ave. and Mount Auburn St.)* to car traffic Sundays from 11AM–7PM April through November.

Arts & Entertainment:

Those with a bent for poetry will want to pay homage to Henry Wadsworth Longfellow, author of *Paul Revere's Ride* and *The Song of Hiawatha*, by visiting his home, the **Longfellow House-Washington Headquarters National Historic Site (6)** *(105 Brattle St., 617-876-4491, www.nps.gov/long; grounds and gardens open daily dawn–dusk, house open June–Oct by guided tour only, call for details)*. Longfellow first resided here as a boarder during a teaching fellowship at Harvard University; when he married Fanny Appleton in 1841, her father purchased the house as a wedding gift for the couple. The house also served as headquarters for General George Washington and the Continental Army while he planned the Siege of Boston from 1775 to 1776. The interior is filled with period furnishings and Longfellow books and memorabilia. After you've been inspired by Longfellow, immerse yourself in contemporary poetry during the weekly poetry slams at **Cantab Lounge (7)**

(738 Massachusetts Ave., 617-354-2685, www.cantab-lounge.com and www.slamnews.com, M–W 8AM–1AM, Th–Sa 8AM–2AM, Su noon–1AM, poetry slam W evenings at 8PM). Poets have three minutes to read their work; the audience judges. Featured poets also perform.

Early in their careers, Joan Baez, Bob Dylan, Tom Rush, and Suzanne Vega played fabled **Club Passim (8)** *(47 Palmer St., 617-492-5300, www.clubpassim.org; box office daily 6:30PM–10PM),* once the influential Club 47, part of the nonprofit Passim Center arts organization dedicated to the cultivation and preservation of folk music. It still attracts a bohemian crowd. The inspired vegetarian café/pizzcria **Veggie Planet ($)** *(617-661-1513, www.veggieplanet.net, daily 11:30AM–10:30PM)* shares the space. And although a "dry" club for more than 50 years, Club Passim now serves wine and beer during shows. "Keeping it reel since 1953," **Brattle Theatre (9)** *(40 Brattle St., 617-876-6837, www.brattlefilm.org; box office opens 30 minutes before the first show of the day)* presents international, classic, and independent films, with a different double feature nearly every day, along with film series featuring specific directors and genres. The nationally acclaimed **American Repertory Theatre (10)** *(64 Brattle St., 617-547-8300, www.amrep.org, Tu–Su noon–5PM, noon–8PM on performance days)* stages dynamic productions of new plays and progressive adaptations of classic works. Its Oberon Stage is known for fringe-style fare.

You could easily spend a day discovering treasures at the **Harvard Museum of Natural History (11)** *(26 Oxford St., 617-495-3045, www.hmnh.harvard.edu, daily 9AM–5PM)*, a three-in-one museum that journeys across thousands of miles and millions of years. In the **Museum of Comparative Zoology**, dinosaurs still rule—at least in terms of popularity with kids—but there are also remarkable mounted displays of mammals, birds, and fish. Talk about bling—the gem collection at the **Mineralogical and Geological Museum** includes a 1,600-pound amethyst. And the **Herbaria Botanical Museum** glass flower gallery is breathtaking. Here, over 3,000 intricate glass models of flowers crafted in Germany from 1886 to 1936 are on display; they were originally a botanical teaching resource that over time became appreciated as art. Admission also includes entry to the **Peabody Museum of Archaeology and Ethnology (12)** *(entrance the Harvard Museum of Natural*

History or at 11 Divinity Ave., 617-496-1027, www.peabody.harvard.edu, daily 9AM–5PM); its Hall of the North American Indian is particularly impressive. So are its collections of Aztec and Mayan stonework, and its fourth floor Oceania exhibit.

These are exciting times at the **Harvard Art Museum (13)** *(32 Quincy St., 617-495-9400 www.artmuseums.harvard.edu, Tu–Sa 10AM–5PM)*. A combination of three museums and four research centers, the building is currently undergoing a major renovation, scheduled to be completed in 2013, which will eventually house the collections of all three

 Harvard Art museums under one roof. The museum is open during construction; the exhibit "Re-View" at the **Arthur M. Sackler Museum** highlights the most important works from each museum. The **Fogg Art Museum** is known for works by medieval masters, 19th-century French artists, Impressionists, and Picasso. The **Busch-Reisinger Museum**, emphasizes art from Teutonic countries. Especially interesting is its collection of modern art from German, Swiss, Austrian, and like cultures. And the focus of the **Sackler Museum** is antiquities from Egypt, Greece, and Italy and treasures from both the Near and Far East.

Exhibits at the **MIT Museum (14)** *(265 Massachusetts Ave., 617-253-5927, http://web.mit.edu/museum, daily 10AM–5PM)* encompass science, technology, architecture, oceanography, and ship design. Check out its jaw-dropping robotics, holographic art, and the intriguing **Innovation Gallery** that showcases current MIT research. Also located nearby is the **MIT List Visual Arts Center** *(20 Ames St., Bldg. E15, 617-253-4680, Tu–W, F–Su noon–6PM, Th noon–8PM)*, showcasing contemporary art, with a permanent collection of over 3,000 prints, photographs, paintings, sculpture, and more.

PLACES TO EAT & DRINK
Where to Eat:

Café Algiers (15) ($) *(40 Brattle St., 617-492-1557, daily 11AM–midnight)* is a hangout that attracts quiet intellectual types. Its Turkish coffee or brewed tea will keep you caffeinated for hours; diners go for the hummus platter. **Border Café (16) ($)** *(32 Church St., 617-864-6100, www.bordercafe.com, M–Th 11AM–1AM, F–Sa 11AM–2AM, Su noon–midnight)* has plentiful platters of Tex-Mex standards—enchiladas, burritos, and quesadillas. Large, strong drinks and unlimited supplies of warm nachos and fresh salsa will keep everybody happy. Fresh, locally grown organic produce makes all the difference at **Henrietta's Table (17) ($$)** *(Charles Hotel, 1 Bennett St., 617-661-5005, www.henriettastable.com, M–F 6:30AM–11AM, noon–3PM, 5:30PM–10PM, Sa 7AM–11AM, noon–3PM, 5:30PM–10PM, Su 7AM–10:30AM, noon–3PM, 5:30PM–10PM)*. Its haute crunchy New England cuisine is served in a laid-back atmosphere. Sip a "Sage Margarita" or splurge on the cranberry pear cake with molasses sauce and pear chutney (hey, it's heart-healthy). Spoil yourself at decadently pink **Upstairs on the Square (18) ($$$)** *(91 Winthrop St., 617-864-1933, www.upstairsonthesquare.com; Monday Club daily 11AM–1AM; Soiree Dining Room Tu–Th 5PM–10PM, F–Sa 5:30PM–11PM)*, either at the more casual **Monday Club Bar** downstairs or the sophisticated **Soirée Room** upstairs. During the day, the Monday Club is the place for a "Restorative Beverage"—hot cocoa with house-made marshmallows and vanilla Chantilly cream. Or do afternoon tea: choose from traditional, zebra, or grand peppermint tea. Here for drinks? Order a plate of "Hot Dates"—dates stuffed with a marcona almond and wrapped in bacon.

Thanks to its smokin' barbecue and ably grilled seafood, meat and fish lovers leave famous **East Coast Grill and Raw Bar (19) ($$)** *(1271 Cambridge St., 617-491-6568, www. eastcoastgrill.net, M–Th 5:30PM–10PM, F–Sa 5:30PM– 10:30PM, Su 11AM–2:30PM, 5:30PM–10PM)* deliriously happy. The wine list is affordable, too. Cambridge is the epicenter of area Indian restaurants. Tried and true, **India Pavilion (20) ($)** *(17 Central Square, 617-547-7463, www.royalbharatinc.com, daily noon–11PM)* is one of the area's first Indian restaurants and still serves one of the best (and least expensive) Indian lunch buffets. Another exotic option: Afghani restaurant **Helmand (21) ($$)** *(143 First St., 617-492-4646, www.helmandrestaurantcambridge. com, Su–Th 5PM–10PM, F–Sa 5PM–11PM)*. A customer favorite: lamb lawand—leg of lamb sautéed with onion, tomatoes, garlic, mushrooms, cilantro, yogurt, and spices, served with sautéed spinach and challow rice. Everything is accompanied by fresh-baked naan flatbread from the clay-oven tandoor.

Sightseeing burnout? Ice cream from **Toscanini's (22) ($)** *(899 Main St., 617-491-5877, www.tosci.com, M–Sa 8AM–11PM, Su 10AM–11PM)*, a Cambridge institution, is a surefire antidote. Expect intense and unconventional flavors, like khulfee, cake batter, gingersnap molasses, green tea, and Guinness. Close to the sprawling MIT campus, the area around Kendall Square is home to a large number of labs and high-tech companies—along with a burgeoning restaurant scene. **Area Four (23) ($-$$)** *(500 Technology Square, 617-758-4444, www.areafour.com, café M–F 7AM–6PM, Sa–Su 9AM–5PM, restaurant M–W 11:30AM–10PM, Th–F 11:30AM–11PM, Sa 10:30AM–11PM, Su 10:30AM–2PM)* caters to worker bees and foodies with glorious scones and coffee in the morning, artisanal sandwiches at noon, and an after-work bar scene that overflows into the dining room in the evening. Break bread over a good book or political discussion at **Darwin's Ltd. (24) ($)** *(148 Mt. Auburn St., 617-354-5233, www.darwinsltd.com, M–Sa 6:30AM–9PM, Su 7AM–7PM)*, a Harvard Square café with a loyal following for its gourmet sandwiches, homemade soups, and salads.

Located in the shadow of Harvard Yard, **Mr. Bartley's Burger (25) ($)** *(1246 Massachusetts Ave., 617-354-6559, www.mrbartley.com, M–Sa 11AM–9PM, cash only)* is a local institution, famous for its burgers, onion rings, and frappes—what New Englanders call milk shakes!

For a first-rate French repast, head to **Sandrine's (26) ($$)** *(8 Holyoke St., 617-497-5300, www.sandrines.com, M–Th 11:30AM–2:30PM, 5:30PM–9:30PM, F–Sa 11:30AM–2:30PM, 5:30PM–10PM, Su 5:30PM–9PM)*. The emphasis here is on the cuisine of the Alsace region and the specialty of the house, the *flammekueche*—a wood-oven baked flatbread with white cheese and caramelized onions—makes a perfect shareable appetizer.

At **Catalyst ($$)** *(300 Technology Square, 617-576-3000, www.catalystrestaurant.com, M–Th 11AM–2:30PM, 5PM–10PM, F 11AM–2:30PM, 5PM–11PM, Sa 5PM–11PM, Su 5PM–10PM)*, the open kitchen is the centerpiece. Chef-owner William Kovel has created a comfortable yet stylish industrial setting in which to enjoy New American cuisine. The chicken liver mousse is a standout starter, and you can't go wrong with the roasted cod with bacon and mussels.

Convenient to visitors of the **Mount Auburn Cemetery (4)**, **Sofra Bakery and Cafe ($)** *(1 Belmont St., 617-661-3161, www.sofrabakery.com, M 8AM–5:30PM, Tu–F 8AM–7PM, Sa–Su 8AM–6PM)* is a wonderful spot to sample Eastern Mediterranean cuisine; there are carefully composed mezze like whipped celery root with almonds and garlic, green olive and walnut salad, and beet tzatzki. If you love cupcakes—and who doesn't—you have to stop at **Sweet (27)** *(Zero Brattle St., 617-547-2253, www.sweetcupcakes.com, Su–Tu 11AM–9PM, W–Sa 11AM–10PM)*, named "Boston's Best Cupcakes" three years running by the *Improper Bostonian*. They have three other locations in Boston.

Kids:

Regional pizza chain **Bertucci's (28) ($)** *(21 Brattle St., 617-864-4748, www.bertuccis.com, Su–Th 11AM–10PM, F–Sa 11AM–11PM)* serves very good brick-oven pizzas, pastas, and entrées (with must-try hot rolls) at prices that are easy on the family budget. Kids like that they get a small piece of pizza dough to play with while they wait.

Bars & Nightlife:

Attracting the likes of Branford Marsalis, Chick Corea, and Joshua Redman, elegant **Regattabar (29)** *(Charles Hotel, 3rd fl., 1 Bennett St., 617-395-7757, www.regatta barjazz.com, check Web site for schedule)* is one of New England's top jazz clubs. Sip a "Blue Rhythm" and enjoy a tidbit from its light-snack menu as you enjoy views of **Harvard Square (1)**. Can't merengue? No more excuses! Dance instructors will show you how to sizzle on the floor in the second-floor dance hall at **Ryles Jazz Club (30)** *(212 Hampshire St., 617-876-9330, www.rylesjazz.com; showtimes vary, box office Tu–Su 5PM–9PM, closed M)*. The first floor features live music—smooth jazz, world, and funk by national artists, along with the Ryles Jazz Orchestra. Reserve in advance for the Sunday jazz brunch. You can't beat **Bukowski's Tavern (31)** *(1281 Cambridge St., 617-497-7077, Th–Sa 11:30AM–2AM, Su–W 11:30AM–1AM)* for suds and pub grub. Named after the cantankerous Beat-era poet, it offers 99 bottles of beers on the wall (the uncertain may ask barkeeps to spin the "Wheel of Indecision"), a basic lunch and dinner menu, and a popular weekday burger special. Cash only. The **Middlesex Lounge (32)** *(315 Massachusetts Ave., 617-868-6739, www.middlesexlounge.us, M–W 11:30AM–1AM, Th–F 11:30AM–2AM, Sa 5PM–2AM)* is a low-key nightclub that draws a hipster crowd that likes to dance. **Hong Kong (33)** *(1238 Massachusetts Ave., 617-864-5311, www.hongkongharvard.com, Su–W 11:30AM–2AM, Th 11:30AM–2:30AM, F–Sa 11:30AM–3AM)* may be hokey—lots of combination plates and dishes with pineapple—but many an undergrad has had their first

scorpion bowl experience here.
Flat-Top Johnny's (34) *(1 Kendall Square, Bldg. 200, 617-494-9565, www.flattop johnnys.com, Th–F noon–1AM, Sa–Su 3PM–1AM)* caters to billiards buffs with a dozen tournament-sized tables. Up-and-coming local, regional, and nearly-national bands play **Middle East (35)** *(472-480 Massachusetts Ave., 617-864-*

3278, www.mideastclub.com; hours vary), boasting three live-music venues and three restaurants. Its **Corner** space offers jazz and acoustic sounds and features belly dancing on Sundays.

WHERE TO SHOP

A plethora of off-beat, independent shops keep Cambridge cool, despite an influx of mainstream chains. Aspiring hipsters haunt **Hootenanny at the Garage (36)** *(36 JFK St., 617-864-6623, M–Th 11AM–9PM, F–Sa 11AM–10PM, Su noon–8PM)*, featuring a sizable selection of men's and women's clothing and accessories that run the gamut from basic (Levis, Dickies), to designer (Fred Perry), to Goth/punk (Tripp NYC). Vintage clothing hounds and those needing costumes shop **Garment District (37)** *(200 Broadway, 617-876-5230, www. garmentdistrict.com, Su–F 11AM–8PM, Sa 9AM–8PM)*. You can literally dig for bargains on the first floor—clothes in piles are sold for $1.50 a pound. The friendly people "with no common scents" at **Colonial Drug (38)** *(49 Brattle St., 617-864-2222, www.colonialdrug.com, M–F 8AM–7PM, Sa 8AM–6PM)* (not a drugstore at all) stock

more than 1,000 retro and hard-to-find fragrances and classic body care products, like tooth powders and shaving brushes. No credit cards. Mouse- and penguin-shaped signature chocolates at **L. A. Burdick (39)** *(52-D Brattle St., 617-491-4340, www.burdickchocolate.com, Su–Th 8AM–9PM, F–Sa 8AM–10PM)* are especially charming, but all its artisanal sweets and pastries are wonderful. Stop in for a coffee or hot chocolate. **Black Ink (40)** *(5 Brattle St., 866-497-1221, www.blackinkboston.com, M–Sa 10AM–8PM, Su 11AM–7PM)* is packed with great home décor and gift discoveries, from a yellow bird soy sauce pitcher to a tabletop twine holder to clover seed for the garden. Inspire academic greatness—shop member-owned **Harvard Coop (41)** *(1400 Massachusetts Ave., 617-499-2000, www.thecoop.com, M–Sa 9AM–10PM, Su 10AM–9PM)*. Open to the public, this is the place to get most anything emblazoned with Harvard logos—mugs, hoodies, teddy bears, sterling silver Tiffany baby cups, hardwood chairs, and more. You'll also find textbooks, fiction, educational games and toys, and school supplies. Note: Yes, it's pronounced coop (rhymes with scoop). Readers with an international perspective will appreciate the selection of newspapers and magazines at landmark **Out of Town News (42)** *(kiosk at Harvard Sq., 617-354-1441, Su–Th 8AM–10PM, F–Sa 6AM–11PM)*. They'll also like **Schoenhof's (43)** *(76A Mt. Auburn St., 617-547-8855, www.schoenhofs.com, M–W, F–Sa 10AM–6PM, Th 10AM–8PM, closed Su)*, offering North America's largest stock of foreign-language books, including learning materials for over 700 languages and dialects, plus fiction, nonfiction, and children's books in 50 languages. The venerable **Grolier Poetry Book Shop (44)** *(6 Plympton St., 617-547-4648, www.grolierpoetrybookshop.org, Tu–W 11AM–7PM, Th–Sa 11AM–6PM)* has dealt in the work of poets renowned and obscure since 1927.

Kids:

Curious George (45) *(1 JFK St., www.thecuriousgeorge store.com)* features two fun floors of Curious George-themed products, children's literature, and quality toys. **The Million Year Picnic (46)** *(99 Mt. Auburn St., 617-492-6763, www.themillionyearpicnic.com, M 10AM–9PM, Tu 11AM–7PM, W 11AM–10PM, Th–Sa 10AM–10PM, Su 11AM–9PM)* has issues, especially back issues, of popular comics, graphic novels, and indie comics.

WHERE TO STAY

The Charles Hotel (47) *($$$$)* *(1 Bennett St., 617-864-1200, www.charleshotel.com),* located in the heart of **Harvard Square (1)**, contrasts goose-down country quilts, Shaker-inspired furniture, and its lobby library with the latest in hotel room technology—Bose radios, iPod docking stations, flat-screen TVs, even an LCD television screen integrated into the bathroom mirror. **Le Meridien Cambridge-MIT (48)** *($$)* *(20 Sidney St., 617-577-0200, wwwstarwoodhotels. com)* assures techie guests comfort and productivity with ergonomically-designed furniture, wireless and

high-speed Internet access in rooms and public spaces, and laptop-sized in-room safes. The hotel's rooftop garden is a peaceful spot to relax. The decor at **Hotel Marlowe (49)** **($$$)** *(25 Edwin H. Land Blvd., 617-868-8000, www.hotelmarlowe.com)*—purple-and-gold crushed velvet, fake fur, and leopard prints—is fun but a bit funky for Boston. This boutique hotel's unique amenities include complimentary wine hour every evening (which might include a meet-the-author event), guest bicycles (perfect for exploring Cambridge), and access to the Observatory of the **Museum of Science** *(see page 61)* across the street and its telescopes. Don't forget its VIP (Very Important Pets) amenities available for both cats and dogs! An indoor/outdoor pool and proximity to the Science Museum and the CambridgeSide Galleria Mall (with over 100 shops and a food court), makes **Royal Sonesta Hotel (50) ($$$)** *(40 Edwin H. Land Blvd., 617-806-4200, www.royalsonestaboston.com)* a family favorite. A riverside setting offers great views of Cambridge and Boston, and its free shuttle will transport you to attractions on either side of the river. The hotel has an eclectic array of contemporary art. Stop by the hotel's casual **ArtBar ($$)** *(617-806-4122)* for a full breakfast buffet, lunch, or dinner. Its Italian-influenced **restaurant dante ($$-$$$)** *(617-497-4200, www.restaurantdante.com, lunch May–Sep M–F 11:30AM–2:30PM, M–Th 5:30PM–10PM, F–Sa*

5:30PM–11PM, *Su* 5PM–9PM) was named a *Bon Appetit* "Hot 10" U.S. restaurant. Chef Dante de Magistris is a master of classic Southern Italian fare, with all the pasta made in-house. For dessert, order *panna cotta* with wine-soaked pears.

"The sun goes down over Cambridge with as much apparent interest as if he were a Harvard graduate: possibly he is...."

—*William Dean Howells*

chapter 9

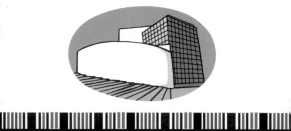

STREETCAR SUBURBS—
DORCHESTER,
JAMAICA PLAIN,
& BROOKLINE

STREETCAR SUBURBS— DORCHESTER, JAMAICA PLAIN, & BROOKLINE

Places to See:

Dorchester

1. JOHN F. KENNEDY PRESIDENTIAL LIBRARY AND MUSEUM ★
2. Franklin Park Zoo

Jamaica Plain

3. Arnold Arboretum
4. Samuel Adams Brewery

Brookline

5. John F. Kennedy National Historic Site
6. Larz Anderson Auto Museum

By the latter half of the 1800s, streetcars made it possible for middle-class Bostonians to work in the city and live in newly developed residential areas outside downtown. Many of these "streetcar suburbs," such as Dorchester, Jamaica Plain, and Brookline, now offer rewarding attractions of their own.

★ *Top Pick*

DORCHESTER

• SNAPSHOT •

Dorchester, settled in 1630 (a month before Boston), is one of America's oldest communities. It's also the site of many U.S. "firsts"—the first water and powder mills, first chocolate factory, first supermarket, first town meeting, and first town to support a public school by taxation. Home to residents of Vietnamese, African, Cape Verdean, Irish, Caribbean, and Latin American descent, the suburb is the site of the University of Massachusetts Boston campus and *The Boston Globe*.

★JOHN F. KENNEDY PRESIDENTIAL LIBRARY AND MUSEUM (1)
Red Line to JFK/UMASS Station, then free JFK Shuttle Bus to Museum

TOP PICK! Step back in time to the Camelot years at the **John F. Kennedy Presidential Library and Museum** *(Columbia Point, Dorchester, 617-514-1600, www.jfklibrary.org, daily 9AM–5PM),* the official library of the charismatic 35th president. The striking I. M. Pei–designed glass-and-white concrete building is set on a picturesque, 10-acre waterfront park planted with pines and wild roses evoking JFK's beloved Cape Cod. The president's 26-foot sailboat *Victura* is displayed from May to October. Administered by the National Archives and Records Administration, the library's collection of historical materials chronicles

mid-20th century politics and John F. Kennedy's life and presidency, as well as the influence of first lady Jacqueline Kennedy on American culture.

The library's introductory film, depicting Kennedy's early life, features narration by JFK himself. Visitors experience a "you-are-there" feeling as they view life-sized replicas of the president's Oval Office, the TV set of the famous Kennedy-Nixon debate, and other rooms; the multimedia exhibits (many furnished with declassi-fied photographs and documents of the time) chronicle the events that defined the Kennedy presidency, includ-ing space exploration, the Cuban missile crisis, and the civil rights movement.

The library is also the repository of the **Ernest Hemingway Collection**, the most comprehensive body of Hemingway material available in one place. Mary Hemingway and Jacqueline Kennedy corresponded in 1968 and arranged for the writer's papers to be donated to  the library. Open to scholars and researchers as well as the general public (by appointment), the holdings com-prise manuscripts and audiovisual and documentary materials. The JFK Library **Museum Store** *(617-514-1605 or 1-866-JFK-1960, ext. 41605, www.jfklibrary. org/store)* offers a range of patriotic, Irish, and Kennedy-related books, DVDs, CDs, china, jewelry, prints, and apparel. The **Museum Café** *(entrance level)* offers beverages and light meals.

Just across from the library, the Massachusetts Archives' **Commonwealth Museum** *(220 Morrissey Blvd., Dorchester, 617-727-9268, www.sec.state.ma.us/mus/ museum/index.htm, M–F 9AM–5PM)* features a permanent exhibit, "Our Common Wealth: The Massachusetts Experiment in Democracy," with interactive displays, an early Massachusetts "look and feel," and treasures on display from the archive vaults.

FRANKLIN PARK ZOO (2)
Orange Line to Forest Hills Station or Red Line to Andrew Station, then Bus 16

Part of Frederick Law Olmsted's Emerald Necklace *(see page 15)*, 520-acre **Franklin Park** *(bet. Dorchester, Jamaica Plain, and Forest Hills, 617-635-4505, www.cityofboston.gov/parks, daily dawn–dusk)* (named after Benjamin Franklin) is the largest in Boston and is considered the park system's crown jewel. The park has bridle paths, a well-regarded golf course, and playing fields, but is best known as the site of the **Franklin Park Zoo** *(1 Franklin Park Rd., Dorchester, 617-541-LION, www. zoonewengland.com, Apr–Sep M–F 10AM–5PM, Sa–Su 10AM–6PM, Oct– Mar daily 10AM–4PM)*. Here you can

say hello to Bengal tiger "Anala" and white tiger "Luther." Enjoy the monkey business at the **Tropical Forest**, take in the majestic African lions in **Kalahari Kingdom**, and watch giraffes and zebras roam freely at **Giraffe Savannah**. Twin rare red pandas, born July 4, 2011 and appropriately named "Yanhua" (fireworks in Chinese) and "Duli" (independence), make an adorable case for the importance of endangered species survival. The stroller set favors the **Franklin Farm** petting zoo.

Dorchester dining options might include **224 Boston Street ($$)** *(224 Boston St., Dorchester, 617-265-1217, www.224bostonstreet.com, Su–Th 5:30PM–10PM, F–Sa 5:30PM–11PM)*, serving American cuisine with a flair, like cider-braised pork shanks with  apple cabbage slaw and mashed potatoes. Cozy **Ashmont Grill ($$)** *(555 Talbot Ave., Dorchester, 617-825-4300, www.ashmontgrill.com, Su 10AM–3PM, 4PM–10PM, M–Th 5PM–10PM, F 5PM–11PM, Sa 10AM–3PM, 5PM–11PM, SU 10AM–3PM, 4PM–10PM)* is known for hip yet homey comfort food, like baked macaroni with three cheeses and bistro-style half-roast chicken with vegetables.

Celtic, Liverpool, New Castle United, or Manchester City? Follow your favorite football club at **The Banshee ($)** *(934 Dorchester Ave., Dorchester, 617-436-9747, www.bansheeboston.com, M–F 10AM–1AM, Sa–Su 8AM–1AM)*, a pub that's popular with the UMass crowd. Try the Dublin bangers or the 10–ounce Angus burger with Irish bacon and Irish cheddar cheese.

JAMAICA PLAIN

• SNAPSHOT •

Jamaica Plain, affectionately known as "J.P.," is one of Boston's most interesting neighborhoods. A modern enclave of young families, Latinos, and a gay and lesbian population, J.P. was founded by Puritans and was one of America's first streetcar suburbs. Defined by several Emerald Necklace parks, including Arnold Arboretum, Jamaica Pond, and Olmsted Park, this verdant district has been called the "Eden of America."

ARNOLD ARBORETUM (3)

Orange Line to Forest Hills Station,
Bus 39 to Custer Street

One of the city's hidden gems, the **Arnold Arboretum** (*125 Arborway, Jamaica Plain, 617-524-1718, www. arboretum.harvard.edu, grounds open daily sunrise–sunset, Visitor Center open M–F 9AM–4PM, Sa 10AM–4PM, Su noon–4PM*), a Harvard University research institution, comprises 265 acres of wooded parkland and landscaped grounds featuring thousands of ornamental plantings. Every season offers something special. The **Bradley Rosaceous Collection** (*Meadow Rd. just inside the Forest Hills Gate*) is a visitor favorite. The **Larz Anderson Bonsai Collection** (*bet. the Dana Greenhouses and the Leventritt Shrub and Vine Garden, on view Apr–Nov*) is one of North America's oldest. The **Lilac Collection** is world famous—more than 400 specimens here flower in May; their fragrance draws Bostonians for the arboretum's Lilac Sunday *(see page 19)*. Mountain laurels, azaleas, and rhododendrons also bloom in late spring, and the grounds blaze with color once again in the fall. **Hemlock Hill**, an indigenous stand of hemlock forest, has an almost magical feeling. The variety of pine trees along **Conifer Path** is unexpectedly interesting. The arboretum is vast and meant to be explored on foot; pick up a map at the **Hunnewell Visitor Center** *(near Arborway Gate)* to guide your wanderings. Free docent-led tours are offered on select dates; check Web site for information.

SAMUEL ADAMS BREWERY (4)
Orange Line toward Forest Hills Station,
exit at Stony Brook

Samuel Adams is Boston's—and America's—premium beer brand. Part history lesson, part brewery tour, a visit to the **Samuel Adams Brewery** *(30 Germania St., Jamaica Plain, 617-368-5080, www.samueladams.com/contact_tour.aspx, M–Th, Sa 10AM–3PM, F 10AM–5:30PM)* is lots of fun. The guides are hilarious, and yes, there are free samples of the company's popular brands (and sometimes new test brews) in the tasting room at tour's end. The tour is open to all ages, but you must have proper ID to imbibe.

The Sam Adams Brewery Tour is among Boston's most popular attractions, so you may have to wait. Next door, funky **Ula Café ($)** *(284 Armory St., 617-524-7890, www.ulacafe.com, M–F 7AM–7PM, Sa–Su 8AM–7PM)* is especially convenient and sells artisan coffees, pastries, and creative lunch items like lemon chickpea soup and a sweet potato sandwich on semolina bread. Tip: Certain Samuel Adams "one-off" brands are available to the public only at **Doyle's Café**. *(3484 Washington St., Jamaica Plain, 617-524-2345, www.doylescafeboston. com, daily 9AM–12:30AM)*, located near the brewery. Founded in 1882, this is one of the oldest Irish pubs in the U.S.; decades of memorabilia line its dark walls. Most every Boston politico drops in for a bite or a pint here on the campaign trail.

After dinner, indulge at **J. P. Licks ($)** *(659 Centre St., Jamaica Plain, 617-524-6740; www.jplicks.com, daily 6AM–midnight)*, a local chain known for its award-winning homemade ice cream. Fun specialty flavors like fresh peach (summer) and chai (winter) are rotated monthly from its 200-flavor library.

BROOKLINE

• SNAPSHOT •

Originally dubbed "Muddy River" a few centuries back, the upscale suburb of Brookline was part of Boston until 1705, when its town was independently incorporated. Its name comes from the brooks that serve as town line boundaries. Brookline is famed for its **Country Club**, one of the five charter clubs responsible for starting the United States Golf Association. The club hosted the legendary 1913 U.S. Open won by the then unknown amateur Francis Ouimet (subject of the book and film *The Greatest Game Ever Played*). Frederick Law Olmsted's **Fairsted** *(99 Warren St., 617-566-1689, www.nps.gov/frla, grounds open daily dawn–dusk)*, his home and the world's first professional landscape design office, is also located in Brookline; this National Park-operated site has recently reopened to the public after extensive renovations. Ranger-led tours of the design office and grounds are offered in season. Check Web site for times.

JOHN F. KENNEDY NATIONAL HISTORIC SITE (5)
*Green "C" Cleveland Circle Trolley to
Coolidge Corner Station or
Bus 66 from Harvard Square to Coolidge Corner*

The **John F. Kennedy National Historic Site** *(83 Beals St., Brookline, 617-566-7937, www.nps.gov/jofi, house open May–Oct W–Su 9:30AM–5PM)*, where JFK was born in 1917, is located on a quiet residential street in Brookline. The Kennedy family lived here from 1914 through 1920. Rose Kennedy personally chose the museum furniture and memorabilia to reflect life as it was when the family occupied the home. National Park Service ranger-led tours of the site are available throughout the day; self-guided tours also available.

LARZ ANDERSON AUTO MUSEUM (6)
*Green "D" Line to Cleveland Circle T Station
Bus 51 to Newton Street*

Located on a gorgeous estate owned by the city of Brookline, the **Larz Anderson Auto Museum** *(Larz Anderson Park,*  *15 Newton St., Brookline, 617-522-6547, www.larz anderson.org, Tu–Su 10AM–4PM)* exhibits America's oldest collection of automobiles. Based on the original collection of horseless carriages and vintage motorcars purchased by ambassador Anderson and his socialite wife, Isabel Weld Perkins—starting with an 1899 Winton Runabout—the museum displays classic American and European models, automobile memorabilia, and antique bicycles. On weekends from May through October, the museum hosts themed lawn events, too, featuring German or Italian cars, American muscle cars, motorcycles, and more.

Fill 'em up at **Rubin's Kosher Restaurant Delicatessen ($)** *(500 Harvard St., Brookline, 617-731-8787, www.rubins boston.com, Su 8AM–8:30PM, M–Th 9AM–9PM, F 9AM–2PM, closed Sa)*, a bite of the Big Apple in Boston. Its "large" and "overstuffed" kosher combo sandwich selection includes "The Carnegie" (turkey), the "Wall Street" (corned beef, tongue, coleslaw, and Russian dressing), and the "Manhattan" (corned beef, hot Romanian pastrami, and chopped liver). **Rami's ($)** *(324 Harvard St., Brookline, 617-325-2355, www.ramisboston.com, Su–Th 10AM–10PM, F 10AM–3PM, closed Sa)* packs its falafel sandwiches with hummus, pickles, red cabbage, and really hot sauce. The amazing savory and sweet crepes at **Paris Creperie ($)** *(278 Harvard St., 617-232-1770, www.pariscrepe.com, Su–Th 8AM–10PM, F–Sa 8AM–11PM)* are a welcome change for a quick lunch or snack. **Anna's Taqueria ($)** *(446 Harvard St., Brookline, 617-277-7111, www.annastaqueria.com, daily 8AM–11PM, cash only)* serves tasty burritos, tacos, and quesadillas.

chapter 10

EXCURSIONS OUTSIDE
BOSTON

EXCURSIONS OUTSIDE BOSTON

Places to See:
1. Concord, MA
2. Old Sturbridge Village, Sturbridge, MA
3. Salem, MA
4. Plymouth. MA
5. Newport, RI
6. Provincetown, MA

"Hub of the universe," one of Boston's nicknames, may be an overstatement, but Massachusetts's capital certainly is New England's hub. Its convenient location makes it easy to take day trips throughout the region. Rent a car and get away!

CONCORD, MA (1)
Route 2 (average drive time: 30 minutes)

Concord is a picturesque New England town and a history buff's delight. Start your visit at **Concord Museum** *(200 Lexington Rd., Concord, 978-369-9763, www. concordmuseum.org, Jan–Mar M–Sa 11AM–4PM, Su 1PM–4PM, Apr–Dec M–Sa 9AM–5PM, Su noon--5PM; June–Aug, open Su 9AM–5PM)* to get an overview of the community's rich history as a Native American settlement, the site of one of the Revolution's earliest battles, and as a 19th-century intellectual and literary center. Its **Museum Shop** *(978-369-5477)* stocks lots of fun items—tricorn hats, penny candy, 1775 lanterns, powder horns, and more.

For many, **Minute Man National Park** (*174 Liberty St., Concord, 978-369-6993, www.nps.gov/mima, sunrise–sunset*) is hallowed ground. The Visitor Center (*spring–fall daily 9AM–5PM, late Oct–Nov closes at 4PM*) offers the multimedia program "Road to Revolution" (shown every 30 minutes), describing the events of April 19, 1775, when the British marched on Concord. Explore **Battle Road Trail**, and tour **Hartwell Tavern** (*late spring–fall, daily 9:30AM–5:30PM*) and **The Wayside: Home of Authors** (*late spring–fall by guided tour only, W–Su 10AM, 11AM, 1PM, 2PM, 3PM, 4:30PM*). Look across the re-created **North Bridge** (*bridge visitor center spring–fall, daily 9AM–5PM, Nov closes at 4PM, check park Web site for winter hours*)—it's easy to imagine the encounter between the redcoats and the rebels and "the shot heard 'round the world." Daniel Chester French's famed *Minute Man* statue commemorates the militia men who had to be ready at a minute's notice. Note: Tours and programs are seasonal; check Web site before you go.

Then travel to **Walden Pond State Reservation** (*915 Walden St., Concord, 978-369-3254, http://www.mass.gov/dcr/parks/walden/, daily 8AM–sunset*). It was here that Henry David Thoreau lived for two years in a one-room cabin (a replica is on site) and penned the book *Walden*. Visitors enjoy the tranquil beauty of these woods year-round; hiking trails through the dense forest are well marked. But be warned: Walden Pond is a popular summer swimming spot, and the park closes when capacity is reached—usually by midmorning on a hot day.

Fans of Louisa May Alcott will want to visit her **Orchard House** (*399 Lexington Rd., Concord, 978-369-4118, www.louisamayalcott.org, Apr–Oct M–Sa 10AM–4:30PM, Su 1PM–4:30PM; Nov–Mar M–F 11AM-3PM, Sa 10AM–4:30PM, Su 1PM–4:30PM; closed Jan 1–3 and major holidays*), operated by the Louisa May Alcott Memorial Association. Alcott wrote and set *Little Women* here; visitors say seeing the house is like "walking through the book." Guided tour only. Tip: Check Web site for discount offers before you go. Stop by its **Museum Shop** for Alcott gifts, books, and collectibles.

The **Concord Cheese Shop ($)** (*29 Walden St., Concord, 978-369-5778, www.concordcheeseshop.com, Tu–F 10AM–5:30PM, Sa 9:30AM–5:30PM, closed Su and M*) is a great place to stop for gourmet sandwiches, salads, and entrées. It's primarily a take-out spot, but there are a few tables. You'll find elements of culinary genius at newcomer **80 Thoreau ($$-$$$)** (*80 Thoreau St., Concord, 978-318-0008, www.80thoreau.com, M–Th 5:30PM–10:30PM, F–Sa 5:30PM–11:30PM*), which presents harvest-inspired New American dishes with panache. Try the poached haddock in lobster broth, or grilled quail with bulgur, dates, and pistachios.

For more information on attractions, restaurants, and accommodations, contact the **Concord Chamber of Commerce** (*Visitor Center located at 58 Main St., Concord, 978-369-3120, www.concordchamberofcommerce.org, spring–fall 10AM–4PM, restrooms open year-round 7AM–8PM*).

OLD STURBRIDGE VILLAGE, STURBRIDGE, MA (2)
Routes I-90, 20, & 84 (average drive time: 1 hour)

Located west of Boston, 200-acre **Old Sturbridge Village** *(1 Old Sturbridge Village Rd., Sturbridge, 508-347-3362, www.osv.org, Mar–Oct daily 9:30AM–5PM, Nov–Feb W–Su 9:30AM–4PM)* transports you to rural New England in the 1830s. Actors portray farmers, craftspeople, and townsfolk to interpret and demonstrate everyday tasks, such as butter-making, blacksmithing, bookbinding, rug-making, and musket firing (cover your ears!). Kids can dress up in 19th-century clothes, tour a one-

room schoolhouse, and see farm animals. Tip: Your ticket admits you into the village for two days within a 10-day period. The **Shops at Sturbridge Village** offer a range of top-quality merchandise, from self-winding wooden tops and replica halfpennies to heirloom seeds and period fabrics. And if all the history makes you hungry, stop by the **Bullard Tavern ($)** cafeteria for soup and a sandwich. The **Grant Store ($)** and **Village Café ($)** offer hot and cold beverages and fresh baked goods, including homemade cookies!

SALEM, MA (3)

Route 1A (average drive time: 30 minutes)
Ferry from Boston (average travel time via ferry 1 hr.)

As a major seaport city, three centuries of trade made Salem rich, but the witch trials of 1692 made it famous. "Stop by for a spell" at the **Salem Witch Museum** *(Washington Sq. N., Salem, 978-744-1692, www.salemwitchmuseum.com, daily 10AM–5PM, July–Aug open until 7PM, extended hours in Oct)*, located in a former church. Its audiovisual presentation of the story of the trials manages to be (appropriately) scary, fun, and educational. The museum also traces the history of witches, witchcraft, and witch hunts through the ages, and examines modern perceptions about witches.

Founded in 1799, the world-class **Peabody Essex Museum** *(East India Square, Salem, 978-745-9500, www.pem.org, Tu–Su and holiday Mondays 10AM–5PM)* is America's oldest continuously operating museum. Committed to creative education, the PEM has been named one of America's "Top 10 Art Museums for Kids." A recent expansion and renovation spectacularly showcases its vast collections of art, architecture, maritime objects, and photographs (over two million items!) from New England, Native America, Asia, Africa, Oceania, China, Japan, and India. Its sizable campus includes parks, gardens, and

24 historic properties. A highlight: **Yin Yu Tang**, the reconstructed, 200-year-old home of a Chinese merchant, the only Qing Dynasty home of its kind outside China. The museum's glass-roofed **Atrium Café ($)** is a nice spot for a quick bite between exhibits. The **Garden Restaurant ($-$$)** is open for lunch from April–October. The menu highlights New American cuisine like raspberry chicken salad. Weather permitting, enjoy lunch in the Japanese Garden.

And don't miss the venerable **House of the Seven Gables** *(115 Derby St., Salem, 978-744-0991, www.7gables.org, Nov–June 10AM–5PM, July–Oct 10AM–7PM, Oct weekends open until 11PM, closed early Jan)*, the oldest surviving 17th-century wooden mansion in New England. On the grounds of this, the home that inspired Nathaniel Hawthorne's eerie tale, you'll actually find five separate historic structures (including Hawthorne's own birthplace, which was moved here in 1958), plus two Colonial Revival seaside gardens. Locals swear by **Gulu-Gulu Café ($)** *(247 Essex St., Salem, 978-740-8882, www.gulu-gulu.com, Su–Tu 8AM–11PM, W–Sa 8AM–1AM)*, a casual coffeehouse known for great live music and tasty food with a Czech bent.

For more info on Salem sights, lodging, and dining, contact **Destination Salem** *(54 Turner St., Salem, 978-744-3663, www.salem.org).*

PLYMOUTH, MA (4)

Routes 3 and 44 (average drive time: 45 minutes)

The first permanent European settlers in New England arrived at what is now Plymouth, Massachusetts, in 1620 on the ship *Mayflower*. Living history museum **Plimoth Plantation** *(137 Warren Ave., Plymouth, 508-746-1622, www.plimoth.org; most attractions open 9AM–5PM from late Mar–late Nov)* takes you back in time to the world of the English colonists and the native Wampanoag. Wander the English village where skilled, costumed interpreters describe life here in 1627. At the Wampanoag home-site, native and non-native staff discusses culture and history. The plantation's **Mayflower II** *(moored 3 miles away dockside at the State Pier, downtown Plymouth)* is a replica of the ship that brought the Pilgrims from England to the New World. Hear harrowing tales of life at sea from character guides in period dress. And, though the colonists who arrived via the first *Mayflower* never mentioned a "rock" in their writings, the large stone at harbor's edge (under the granite portico) was identified by Elder William Faunce in 1741 as the definitive landing spot of the Pilgrims. Now **Plymouth Rock** *(Pilgrim Memorial State Park, Water St., Plymouth, 508-747-5360, www.mass.gov/dcr/parks/southeast/plgm.htm)* is a must-see.

Another Plymouth landmark: the **Lobster Hut ($)** *(25 Town Wharf, 508-746-2270, www.lobsterhutplymouth.com, summer daily 11AM–9PM, winter daily 11AM–7PM)*, the place to go for fried fish or boiled lobster. Nothing fancy here—just fresh seafood, a fast-food ambience, and waterfront view. Try a lobster salad roll, or seafood platter for two. In chilly weather, warm up with clam chowder or lobster bisque. Burgers and chicken available, too. Dine in the dining room or enjoy the harbor sights outside under the canopy.

For more information on things to do, restaurants, and accommodations, contact the **Plymouth Visitor Information Center** *(130 Water St., Plymouth, across from Plymouth Harbor, 508-747-7525, www.visit-plymouth.com)*.

NEWPORT, RI (5)
Routes I-93, 24, and 114
(average drive time: 1 hour, 15 minutes)

The seaside city of Newport, Rhode Island, was once the playground of America's wealthiest families. Its summer "cottages" are in fact the grandest of mansions, and 11 of the properties are open to the public. The operating schedule for each property varies seasonally, so be sure to visit the Web site of Newport County's **Preservation Society** *(424 Bellevue Ave., Newport, 401-847-1000, www.newportmansions.org)* for trip-planning information before you go. Tip: Allow at least one-and-one-half hours

 or more per mansion. From Memorial Day through Columbus Day, you can park at the **Newport Visitor Information Center** *(see page 200)* for a small fee ride the **RIPTA (Rhode Island Public Transit Authority)** Yellow Line trolley to the properties.

The spectacular **Breakers** *(44 Ochre Point Ave., open year-round)*, built for the Vanderbilts, is the grandest of the "cottages." The new "Breakers Revealed" self-guided audio tour focuses on the architectural beauty of the home and includes personal accounts from the Vanderbilt children and the Vanderbilt servants. Designed by Richard Morris Hunt, the **Marble House** *(596 Bellevue Ave., open year-round)* is another Vanderbilt mansion, notable for the lavish use of marble both inside and out. Located on the manicured back lawn and overlooking the sea cliffs, the exquisite **Chinese Tea House** *(open Memorial Day weekend–Columbus Day)* is a lovely lunch or snack option. A unique **"behind-the-scenes" tour** at the **Elms** *(367 Bellevue Ave.; open year-round)* takes you through the kitchens, coal cellar, boiler room, wine cellar, third-floor staff quarters, and out onto the roof to see the grounds and the harbor. You can also enjoy lunch at the **Elms Carriage House Café** *(mid-May–mid-Oct 10AM–4PM)*—sandwiches, salads, and snacks are available to purchase. Eat on the terrace and look out over the expansive gardens and imagine life during the Gilded Age.

Houdini once performed for partygoers at **Rosecliff** *(548 Bellevue Ave., open mid-Mar–mid-Nov)*, owned by Nevada silver heiress Theresa Fair Oelrichs. **Chateau-sur-Mer** *(474 Bellevue Ave., open mid-Mar–mid-Nov)* features outstanding examples of High Victorian furnishings and decor. Fanciful **Kingscote** *(253 Bellevue Ave., open mid-May–mid-Oct)* is grand Gothic Revival.

Take a restorative break at the Preservation Society's **Green Animals Topiary Garden** *(380 Corys Ln., Portsmouth,*

401-847-1000, open early May–mid-Oct), comprising formal topiaries, vegetable and herb gardens, orchards, and a Victorian house on seven acres overlooking Narragansett Bay. You'll find privet, yew, and boxwood plants fashioned into 80 whimsical topiary sculptures, including teddy bears, dogs, birds, and an elephant. The earliest date from 1910.

Walk all or part of the three-and-one-half-mile **Cliff Walk** *(beginning at Memorial Blvd., www.cliffwalk.com, daily sunrise–sunset)*, a National Recreation Trail. Enjoy the wildflowers, birds, and magnificent views of the Atlantic and ocean waves crashing against the cliffs. Note: The trail can be rocky and its steep drops hidden by bushes and weeds, including poison ivy. Wear proper shoes and use care.

For more on area sights, accommodations, and dining, contact the **Newport Visitor Information Center** *(23 America's Cup Ave., Newport, 401-849-8048, www.gonewport.com, daily 9AM–5PM)*.

PROVINCETOWN, MA (6)
Ferry from Boston (average travel time: 90 minutes via high-speed ferry, 3 hours regular ferry)

Cape Cod is the spit of land that juts out into the Atlantic from the easternmost part of Massachusetts and is world-famous for its beaches, sand dunes, and salt marshes. Provincetown is the seaside resort on the tip of Cape Cod, "where America begins." "P-town," as it is also known, has a rich colonial history, a whaling and fishing heritage, and an established arts community. A popular gay travel destination, P-town is diverse and inclusive—all are welcome.

You can take a ferry from Boston and be in P-town in as little as 90 minutes. **Bay State Cruise Company** *(200 Seaport Blvd., Boston, 877-783-3779, www.baystatecruises.com)* and **Boston Harbor Cruises** *(1 Long Wharf, Boston, 617-227-4321, www.bostonharborcruises.com)* both offer Boston/Provincetown ferry service from May to October.

Renting a bike is a great way to get around. **P-town Bikes** *(42 Bradford St., Provincetown, 508-487-8735, www.ptownbikes.com, 9AM–6PM in season, May–Oct)* and **Gale Force Bikes** *(144 Bradford St. Extension, Provincetown, 508-487-4849, www.galeforcebikes.com, 8AM–8PM in season, May–Oct)* rent bikes for time periods as short as two hours. Or hire a pedicab from **P-town Pedicabs** *(377 Commercial St., Unit 3-4, Provincetown, 508-487-0660, www.ptownpedicabs.com, May–Oct)*. Part bicycle, part rickshaw, a pedicab is an option that allows you to see and be seen as part of the daily parade that is uniquely P-town.

The **Cape Cod National Seashore** *(508-771-2144, www.nps.gov/caco)* was established in 1961 by President John F. Kennedy, a long-time summer resident here. Forty miles of beaches stretch from the town of Chatham mid-Cape to P-town. The **Province Lands Visitor Center** *(Race Point Rd., 508-487-1256, www.nps.gov/caco, May–Oct daily 9AM–5PM)* should be your first stop. The observation deck affords a 360-degree view of the dunes, the beach, and the

Atlantic Ocean. From here you can access an easy walking trail, a bike trail, and the beaches. Note: Herring Cove Beach is known for nudity. Race Point Beach, at land's end, is wildly beautiful, but the surf is rough.

The **Pilgrim Monument** and **Provincetown Museum** *(High Pole Hill Rd., Provincetown, 508-487-1310, www.pilgrim-monument.org, Apr 1–May 31 daily 9AM–5PM, June 1–Sep 15 daily 9AM–7PM, Sep 16–Nov 30 daily 9AM–5PM)* is a P-town must-see. The *Mayflower* Pilgrims first landed on North American soil in Provincetown before crossing the bay to settle in Plymouth. The 252-foot monument here is the tallest all-granite structure in America. Theodore Roosevelt laid the cornerstone in 1907; as you climb the 116 steps to the top, check out the interior stones donated by cities and towns throughout the U.S. Is your hometown listed here? The next door **Provincetown Museum** highlights the town's *Mayflower* connection and the area's maritime heritage. P-town was—and is—a thriving artist's colony. **Provincetown Art Association and Museum** *(460 Commercial St., 508-487-1750, www.paam.org, Oct–May Th–Su noon–5PM, late May–Sep M–Th 11AM–8PM, F 11AM–10PM, Sa–Su 11AM–5PM)*, established in 1914, showcases the work of artists past and present with P-town associations. As you step off the ferry

at the town pier, you'll spot the fun and fascinating **Expedition *Whydah* Sea-Lab & Learning Center** *(16 Macmillan Wharf, 508-487-8899, www.whydah.com, May, Sep, Oct daily 10AM–5PM, June–Aug daily*

10AM–8PM, closed Nov–Mar). The **Whydah** is a pirate ship that sank off the coast of Cape Cod in 1717; the museum tells its story through its recovered artifacts.

Bubala's ($$) *(183-185 Commercial St., Provincetown, 508-487-0773, www.bubalas.com, May–Oct daily 11AM–11PM)* is as exuberant as P-town. Its outdoor patio is a prime people-watching spot. The menu is casual with an emphasis on seafood, and the fish-and-chips are a deal. Sit outside under the giant awning or in the brightly colored dining room and sample traditional South African casual food at **Karoo Kafe ($)** *(338 Commercial St., 508-487-6630, www.karookafe.com, May–Oct daily 11AM–9PM)*. Dishes like curried beef pot pie blend Indian and British culinary influences, and the menu offers plenty of options for alternative diets. For more information on vacationing in Provincetown and Cape Cod, contact the **Provincetown Chamber of Commerce** *(307 Commercial St., Provincetown, 508-487-3424, www.ptownchamber.com)* or the **Cape Cod Chamber of Commerce Welcome Center** *(junction Rt. 6 and Rt. 132, Hyannis, 508-362-3225, www.capecodchamber.org)*.

INDEX

transportation map

BOSTON TRANSPORTATION MAP

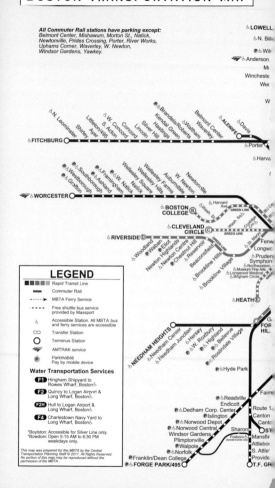

All Commuter Rail stations have parking except:
Belmont Center, Mishawum, Morton St., Natick,
Newtonville, Prides Crossing, Porter, River Works,
Uphams Corner, Waverley, W. Newton,
Windsor Gardens, Yawkey.

LEGEND

▪▪▪▪▪ Rapid Transit Line

— Commuter Rail

----▸ MBTA Ferry Service

----- Free shuttle bus service
provided by Massport

   ᴧ   Accessible Station. All MBTA bus
and ferry services are accessible

∞ Transfer Station

○ Terminus Station

AMTRAK service

Ⓟ Parkmobile
Pay by mobile device

Water Transportation Services

F1 Hingham Shipyard to
Rowes Wharf, Boston&

F2 Quincy to Logan Airport &
Long Wharf, Boston&

F2H Hull to Logan Airport &
Long Wharf, Boston&

F4 Charlestown Navy Yard to
Long Wharf, Boston&

*Boylston: Accessible for Silver Line only.
*Bowdoin: Open 5:15 AM to 6:30 PM
weekdays only.

This map was prepared for the MBTA by the Central
Transportation Planning Staff © 2011. All Rights Reserved.
No portion of this map may be reproduced without the
permission of the MBTA.